PRAISE FOR *NOW, NEAR, NEXT*

"*Now, Near, Next* comes at a time when taking control of our lives and maximizing self-agency is at the forefront of conversations surrounding careers and leadership. By distilling the complexities of what it means to put ourselves first—and tackling the internal and external barriers that hold us back—Cynthia Bentzen-Mercer and Kimberly Rath embody the future and want us all to come along with them."

—DR. MARSHALL GOLDSMITH, Thinkers50 #1 Executive Coach and *New York Times* bestselling author of *The Earned Life, Triggers,* and *What Got You Here Won't Get You There*

"Kimberly and Cynthia have written a book filled with hard-earned leadership and career wisdom perfect for the woman leader who wants to get clear on the next steps in her career and be inspired to take intentional action. Reading this book felt like gaining secret access to years' worth of mentoring sessions from proven leaders."

—KELLI THOMPSON, women's leadership coach, speaker, and author of *Closing the Confidence Gap*

"*Now, Near, Next* is the essential guidebook for women to recognize, articulate, and promote traditional and non-traditional skills to accelerate their careers. Successful leadership for the future of work requires empathy, communication, time management, negotiation, and an ability to make decisions and form consensus in the face of imperfect and incomplete information in a rapidly changing environment."

—HEATHER E. MCGOWAN, Future of Work keynote speaker
and author of *The Adaptation Advantage* + *The Empathy Advantage*

"In *Now, Near, Next,* Cynthia and Kimberly offer a transformative guide for mid-career women, blending practical strategies with personal narratives. From energizing self-agency to navigating life's unexpected turns, the book is full of practical wisdom and proven strategies, serving as a blueprint for realizing a woman's true potential. A must-read!"

—JINGJIN LIU, CEO and founder, ZaZaZu

"Authors Cynthia Bentzen-Mercer and Kimberly Rath courageously confront age-old conditioning that has thwarted women's progress throughout history: women must always be humble. The pervasive notion that women must keep their heads down and work hard has only served to propel the careers of their male peers, who instead are looking ahead and surging forward. Enter *Now, Near, Next,* a pragmatic guide that encourages women to reclaim their autonomy, unapologetically invest in their future, and hype women to do the same."

—ERIN GALLAGHER, CEO + founder, Ella;
creator of Hype Women Movement

"*Now, Near, Next* is an incredible piece that empowers you to take your power back. I was taken aback by vignettes that bring to life the science of personal agency and its profound toll and impact on the lives of women. Cynthia and Kimberly do such a wonderful job of detailing pathways to overcoming the sometimes subconscious stumbling blocks that can make you feel limited. The book leaves you with a sense of ownership of your life. I'm energized by reading it. You will be, too!"

—DAVID SATCHELL, Air Force Command Chief Master Sergeant and author of *Extracting the Leader from Within*

"This book is timely, as many jobs will be impacted by the fourth Industrial Revolution, driven by AI. *Now, Near, Next* is an all-encompassing guide for mid-career women. Each chapter acts as a catalyst for personal and professional excellence, offering not just a reading experience but an interactive journey that fosters self-discovery and empowerment."

—DR. VIRPI TERVONEN, CEO Mindset Coach, RealRelevantResults

"Changing your life for the better isn't always easy, and *Now, Near, Next* means never having to do it alone. There are stories of transformation that can motivate our own, and real-world advice from a diverse range of voices that is implementable for everyone. Sharp, necessary, and the world is ready."

—ANDRÉ STEWART, founder and CEO of InvestFar, Inc. and author of *Epitome of the Mind*

"Accessing and tapping into our fullest potential is more essential than ever—but in this fast-moving world, it's also harder than ever. *Now, Near, Next* empowers us with the guidance we need and speaks to us in ways that are relatable, practical, and meaningful. While the book seeks to activate our self-agency, it also reminds us about the power of our relationships with others. As much about the present as it is about the future, there is a spot for it on every shelf, now and beyond."

—**LORRAINE RISE,** founder and CEO of CareerUpRising and author of *What You Didn't Learn in School*

"Timely, relevant, intensely personal, and expertly written, this book serves as a modern-day GPS for women (and men) who are willing to engage in career reinvention as a way of life. I am making this a must-read for my twin daughters and all the women I know as a guide to life beyond the corporate corridors."

—**REGINALD R. MEBANE,** senior executive and former Mercy board member

"Cynthia and Kimberly have provided clarity on what it takes to stay energized not only in our careers, but in our lives. Through personal experiences and supporting data, they provide guidance and tools for successfully achieving one's own 'Near' and 'Next' with zeal!"

—**BARBARA C. ARCHER,** MBA, CFP,® CLU,® AEP,® CPRC, partner, Hightower Wealth Advisors

"As a mid-career woman, I found Cynthia and Kimberly's book to be a refreshing invitation to focus on myself and seek opportunities to deepen my own self-understanding and intentionality around the dreams I have for my career. As a busy woman, it is easy for a day to turn to a week to turn to a season and year without asking or reflecting on my own direction. Reading *Now, Near, Next* is like a mini professional retreat to reset purpose, focus on a future, and develop a plan that fits within the fullness of the vision I have for all facets of my professional life."

—**JENNA SPECKART,** D. Be., Vice President, Mission & Ethics, Mercy St. Louis

www.amplifypublishing.com

Informatic Illustrations by Muhammad Usman, Founder and Creative Designer, Canvas Crew

For more information, please contact:
Amplify Publishing, an imprint of Amplify Publishing Group
620 Herndon Parkway, Suite 220
Herndon, VA 20170
info@amplifypublishing.com

Library of Congress Control Number: 2023919797
CPSIA Code: PRV1223A
ISBN-13: 978-1-63755-893-5

Printed in the United States

CYNTHIA BENTZEN-MERCER, PHD
AND KIMBERLY K. RATH, MBA

NOW, NEAR, NEXT

A Practical Guide for Mid-Career Women to Move from Professional Serendipity to Intentional Advancement

amplify
an imprint of Amplify Publishing Group

CONTENTS

FOREWORD

By Reimi Marden, CEO,
The Winning Edge, LLC

"READY, SET, GO!" is a phrase you may find oh-so-familiar if you're an ambitious woman like me who has, by default, grown accustomed to living life like it's a race. Even with no intention to live an adrenaline-fueled lifestyle, for women, the demands of our personal lives and careers consume and distract us from being truly present in our *Now*, leaving us ill-equipped to plan our *Near* and, frankly, too exhausted to design our *Next*.

When I was asked to write the foreword for this book, I did not realize how deeply immersed I would be in each chapter. Wow! It was eye-opening, to say the least, and just in time. With thirty-two years in the professional development and corporate training industry, I would marvel at "just-in-time learning" systems—training readily available exactly when and how it is needed by the learner.

Well, here you go. What you hold in your hands today is a missing piece that will bring you clarity and ignite the intentionality that eludes so many of us in our mid-career. What a powerful journey you are about to embark on. Get set for a transformative experience in these interactive pages that you will find uniquely fitting at this exciting junction of your life. Welcome to *Now, Near, Next!*

You will experience an extraordinary kinship with authors **Cynthia Bentzen-Mercer** and **Kimberly K. Rath**, who have brilliantly constructed a blueprint, a metaphorical map, which will guide you. *Now, Near, Next* masterfully combines proven strategies and practical wisdom with heartening narratives of women who have traversed similar paths. These pages unfold as if you were being personally mentored by these two passionate and accomplished women who are paying it forward. Their rich content will meet you where you are and allow you to go at your own pace.

In "Section One: Now—Energize Self-Agency," I heard with new ears, very loud and clear, a rallying call to embrace the power of self-agency—a concept deeply intertwined with initiative, empowerment, responsibility, and, most practically, letting go of the guilt and regret that holds us back. I was reminded of my mid-thirties, when my image-consulting and corporate-training business was soaring at an all-time high, sending me on frequent trips across the country. During this time, my husband and I were eager and struggling to start a family. Ultimately, I began the complex process of fertility treatment. However, the constant travel and demands of my business left so little of me, energetically, emotionally, and physically. It was at this crossroads that I had to stop and chart a new course.

No longer could I let serendipitous circumstances make or break my dream of motherhood. With the help of a personal coach, I began granting myself grace and permission to honor my awakened desire to be a mom. I successfully shifted from living at the speed of life, chasing success in the corporate world, to living a life rooted in holistic self-care and growing a home-based private coaching practice better suited to my hopeful pregnancy. This profound pivot brought a positive energy source where self-care was nonnegotiable and served as a force that surrounded my physical, mental, emotional, and spiritual well-being. Guarding my time, pace, and space protected me through the trials and tribulations of rigorous in vitro fertilization procedures. The financial investment, time commitment, and emotional roller-coaster rides required calm, clarity, and a high level of intentionality. I claimed my vision for my *Near* and was blessed with a miracle child at age thirty-seven.

The formulas shared in "Section Two: Near—Ignite Intentionality" offer even more proven strategies that I can attest will facilitate dreams coming true and potential being actualized. It will illuminate your path and guide you to live into your vision.

This book will prepare you for life's unexpected twists and turns that disrupt and derail. When the proverbial "Universal two-by-four" shatters you to the core and causes you to move (and move fast) in a new direction, you hope that your personal foundation is strong and your community of support is too. Tragedy struck when the love of my life, my husband of twenty-six years then, had a catastrophic stroke, leaving him in a wheelchair, disabled and nonverbal. This ushered in a new and unannounced chapter of full-time caregiving, single-parenting a preteen, and consulting and training throughout the United States and Asia all while managing the inherited responsibilities of my husband's organic apple orchard, which I knew nothing about. I discovered very quickly that asking for help was a superpower.

Cynthia Bentzen-Mercer brilliantly states, *"Women must overcome the feeling of failure if they are not single-handedly doing it all!"* A crash course in asking for help and delegation ensues in this chapter of crisis. Being of Asian descent, I had to dismiss cultural pressure embedded in me to reciprocate, and instead, to learn to graciously receive support when I had nothing to return. I grew to become OK with that and embraced falling short of perfectionism. *Now, Near, Next* speaks to these humbling moments that reframe the superwoman in us and set her straight with grace and proper perspective.

In these nine chapters, you will build a foundation of empowerment that will give a voice to your purpose, which is unshakeable even through difficult times. You will learn to *"listen with your eyes,"* as **Kimberly K. Rath** powerfully prescribes. *"It means looking beyond the limitations imposed by self-doubt and fear and instead, opening our minds to the vast array of possibilities that lie ahead."* This is a skill set women must master to elevate ourselves.

It is truly an honor to share my love for *Now, Near, Next*. This manuscript blessed me immensely, bringing me peace and inspiration during the darkest time of my life after the loss of my beloved husband of thirty-four amazing years. I have the blueprint now to "navigate rerouting" and am actively crafting a new version of my *Next*. Thank you, Cynthia and Kimberly, for this gift of hope for my brightest tomorrow.

To all who are embarking on this life-changing adventure with this masterpiece in hand, do so with awe of the brilliant woman you are today, in your *Now*, and confidently live into the phenomenal version you will be in your *Next*!

Reimi Marden

PREFACE

REMEMBER WHEN LIFE was less complicated, energy was boundless, and time seemed endless? Looking back on the first fifteen years of my career, I was highly intentional. I pursued a Senior Professional in Human Resources certification to expand from training and development to human resources. As a broadcasting and film undergraduate, I later earned an MBA to add business credibility to my résumé and make me more marketable in the publicly traded sector. I sought a position in an organization and industry that broadened my experience and opportunities, even with a more minor role and less pay. Each of those intentional early-career investments paid off and benefited me throughout my mid-career.

However, perhaps like yours, my mid-career has been busy, complicated, and sometimes exhausting. For me, breast cancer, a divorce, and moving my children across the country during my daughter's senior year in high school were just a few life events that occurred while I was pursuing professional aspirations. Although I have worked extremely hard and have been fortunate, throughout most of my mid-career, I was not proactively preparing for what was *Next*. More often, I was reacting to a well-timed opportunity or mid-career restlessness.

During these pivotal career moments, I did enlist many supporters for advice and counsel along the way. Kimberly, a mentor and professional colleague of eighteen years, was always at the top of my call list.

Should I take the job in Las Vegas, in gaming, or the position in Nashville, in restaurants?

How do I transition to an industry I have no experience in?

Which doctorate program makes more sense?

What do you think about writing a book together?

While I had teased this most recent idea several times with her, a call in September 2022 put the dream into action. Energized by the opportunity to elevate women's careers, she agreed. A few months later, we were off to dream big.

A writer's retreat on the sandy beaches of Mexico provided the perfect tranquility to explore our experiences, insights, and perspectives. There, we uncovered what we believe to be a pressing and under-addressed subject—women in mid-career. Namely, women are often so consumed and distracted by the demands of the *Now* that they leave their agency to others by failing to plan for what is *Near* or prepare for what is *Next*. These discoveries launched what has become fundamental to our evidence-based methodology to energize mid-career women to look up, take inventory, make room, and intentionally be present in the **Now**, plan the **Near**, and dream the **Next**!

Kimberly and I began by "drinking our own champagne." Using the *Now, Near, Next* framework, we considered our partnership arrangement and our respective future aspirations. It was at that moment that something powerful was revealed to us. While this book started as another way for me to fulfill a postdoctoral, mid-career lull, it turned out to be the pathway to my *Next*. For

Kimberly, who has begun her encore performance, this book represents a way to pay it forward.

Appreciating our shared passion in the *Now* and *Near*, with attention to our individual plans for what is *Next*, we began to honor and amplify our respective contributions. Kimberly has leaned in as a mentor, coach, supporter, member of my life's board of directors (more on this in chapter five), and thought partner. She developed the infrastructure of our long-term path, conducted critical research, and collaborated as a content expert and editor. With a love of research and a passion for writing, I have given voice to a collection of experiences, learnings, research, and proven strategies.

So, welcome to my *Next*! Throughout nine chapters, you and I will reenergize self-agency and ignite the intentionality that eludes so many women in mid-career. As you journey with me on my *Now*, you will be encouraged to put into practice the evidence-based methods and actions that will actuate your full potential. Together we will move from professional serendipity to intentional advancement, one page at a time!

Cynthia

INTRODUCTION

YOU'VE HEARD THE EXPRESSION "You're the yin to my yang"? That is the best description of the synergy that Kimberly and I have found through this journey together. Although we have joked that it sometimes feels more like the tortoise and the hare.

I am overzealous, eager to move to action, and occasionally impatient. For example, when we signed with Amplify Publishing Group, I downloaded TikTok for the first time, recorded a three-minute ad hoc video announcing our *Now, Near, Next* framework, and shared our excitement to shine a light for mid-career women. Boom, off to the races!

Kimberly, measured, diligent, and focused, followed my post with a gentle text message. She suggested waiting until we received our service mark registration to protect our branding before sharing our concepts with the world, particularly via TikTok. Hmm, details.

Fortunately, like yin and yang, the harmonious balance of our energy has allowed us to amplify the best in each other and leverage our collective sixty-five years of experience. While our respective paths have had many similarities, our journeys have been unique, like those of the many women we interviewed and researched.

Raised in a progressive Mennonite home, Kimberly's formative years juxtaposed traditional family values and her father's encouragement to pursue education and career aspirations regardless of gender. She did just that with the support of her parents, who were the first in their community to marry in a dual-ring ceremony. After graduating from the University of Nebraska-Lincoln and later achieving an MBA from Pepperdine University, Kimberly continued to challenge gender boundaries. She found her passion for understanding and developing human potential.

The cofounder and cochairman of Talent Plus,® Kimberly has spent thirty-five years helping leaders achieve their highest potential through talent-based strategies and solutions. Although her work experience is almost entirely with Talent Plus,® based in Lincoln, Nebraska, her reach and impact are global. Working with a variety of companies around the world, she has dedicated her career to helping others realize their potential and create a leadership legacy.

While I was blessed with amazing parents, it was predominantly my mother who raised me. As a resilient woman who got her GED after leaving high school at seventeen to marry my nineteen-year-old father and give birth to me, my mother set the tone for what was possible. A working mom, she owned and operated several businesses and earned her bachelor's degree at age forty. Working hard and having aspirations as big as our talent was a constant theme of encouragement in our home.

Following my undergraduate degree in broadcasting and film, my initial dream of retiring Barbara Walters as a journalist was set aside when I fell in love with business, leadership, and social psychology—probably for the best, given that Barbara's career carried on for another twenty-five years. Fortunately, my interests have been fulfilled throughout a thirty-year career spanning four states, five companies, multiple relocations, and various industries. Continued education was central to my intrinsic satisfaction and the best way to feed my aspirational appetite. The study of human behavior and seeing talent unleashed became my true north.

As you can see, Kimberly and I have had unique career routes, yet our life experiences have been richly filled with similar successes, failures, moments of pride, and moments of disappointment. Still, we could not be sure that our journey represented women at large. That led us to research the experiences of women throughout their mid-careers.

As a result, this book represents the research, expertise, and experiences that Kimberly and I bring to bear, the voices of nine incredible women whose stories are shared as reflections at the end of each chapter, and quotes and insights gathered from over two hundred women surveyed and thirty women interviewed. Not only did we find immense joy and inspiration in the stories of so many impressive women, but we also found great consistency among their life experiences despite their diverse backgrounds.

Empirical research, our qualitative interviews, and the study of the current literature were conclusive: as women, we experience common themes throughout our mid-career. The root cause of these similarities is collectively societal, self-induced, and habitual. We fill our days and nights doing for others and put off or fail to plan for what is *Near* or prepare for what is *Next*.

Owning and empowering self-agency means taking control of your path ahead. Instead of conforming to social norms or other people's opinions and expectations, you take intentional action to achieve desired outcomes. We debunk the myth that putting your head down and working hard is the best way to realize your fullest potential. Instead, you are challenged to look forward with intentionality, action, and reflection.

As such, this book is intended to energize your self-agency by giving you the tools and the freedom to make room for yourself, bring forethought to your journey, and provide a road map to your *Now, Near, Next*. Throughout the book, we unpack the traps, norms, and burdens that women envelop. While we ground many of the barriers women face in research and experience, we focus on empowering you with the license and tools to reflect, challenge, and pivot.

While numerous credible resources are available to address several concepts in this book, our research revealed that there needs to be more attention paid to the unique challenges and opportunities women face in their mid-career. In three sections, we have outlined a practical approach to energizing your *Now, Near, Next*. Each section has three chapters, which end with a reflection and an action plan.

Section one, "Now—Energize Self-Agency," is intended to set the table for the journey ahead. In these first three chapters, you are invited to let go of the guilt and regret that holds you back, identify your natural talents, and give yourself time and space to dream of what is *Next*. This section is vitally essential to a woman who needs permission, empowerment, encouragement, or a shove to invest in herself without guilt.

Section two, "Near—Ignite Intentionality," moves to action. Chapters four through six reveal the importance of engaging the support of others, proactively investing in professional development, and ensuring that your superpowers remain relevant. Your *Near* may be over six months or a two-year time frame. What is essential is that there is momentum forward and intentional growth.

Section three, "Next—Actualize Potential," addresses spreading your wings, taking risks, and walking with confidence. A *Next*, by definition, has some elements of the unknown. Whether with your current organization, through a move to a new company, or in a transition to something completely new, chapters six through nine encourage you to gain a broad perspective, move forward with courage, and bolster resilience.

Throughout each chapter, I journey with you in what was, for me, real time. Given that it took six months to write the book, life and all of its ebbs and flows continued around me. As fate would have it, chapter nine went through a significant revision just as we were ready to send the manuscript to the publisher. It was this unexpected plot twist that deepened my perspective and conviction to encourage and equip mid-career women to put time and energy into intentional career planning.

As such, this book is designed to energize your journey toward your *Next*. Each chapter builds upon the former, and each section prepares you to move forward. As you read, take the time to reflect, act, and commit at whatever pace works for you. Whether you take it slow and implement one chapter at a time or read cover-to-cover and develop a comprehensive plan, the benefits are gained with momentum.

Included throughout the book are resources and references. Symbols guide you and keep you thinking, doing, and preparing. For those who prefer to journal outside the book, we have created a *Now, Near, Next* Companion Guide, which can be purchased at zealoftheheel.com or wherever books are sold. If you choose not to buy the Companion Guide, you are encouraged to identify another source dedicated to taking notes. You will be invited and reminded to document your commitments along the way.

Symbols are used to guide your journey and keep you thinking, doing, and preparing. You will be invited and reminded to document your commitments along the way.

 Personal Reflection

 Take Immediate Action

 Chart in *Now, Near, Next Blueprint*

If you need inspiration, encouragement, support, empowerment, or even a pointed pump to kick you in the pants, sit back, relax, and dig in! It is your moment to invest unapologetically in yourself, to discover and give life to your *Now, Near, Next!* Moreover, if taking guilt-free time for yourself stresses you out, start with chapter one!

SECTION ONE

Now—Energize Self-Agency

"Section One: Now—Energize Self-Agency" is intended to set the table for the journey ahead. In these first three chapters, you are invited to let go of the guilt and regret that holds you back, celebrate your natural talents, and give yourself time and space to dream of what is next. This section is vitally essential for a woman who needs permission, empowerment, encouragement, or a shove to invest in herself without guilt.

CHAPTER ONE

Take Charge

Embrace the glorious mess that you are.

—**ELIZABETH GILBERT,** American author

THE FLIGHT ATTENDANT ANNOUNCED that we were ready to push back and reminded us to turn off our electronic devices. As I reached to turn off my phone, my son asked with surprise, "You have to turn your phone off?" As I said yes and attempted to explain why, my daughter interrupted with shock and joy. "You mean you'll have to be off your phone the *entire* flight?" Their delight was a painful reminder of the tightrope I had been walking, attempting to balance motherhood and a career.

When we embarked on authoring this book, we theorized that throughout mid-career, women get so bogged down in the daily grind, consumed with the pressure to do it all and the guilt of falling short, that they fail to invest in themselves, plan for what is *Next*, or reflect on their success. Through our interviews with numerous mid-career women, a survey of over three hundred female professionals, and evidence-based research, our assumptions were crystallized. We discovered that exercising personal agency—a feeling of control of actions and circumstances expressed through intentionality, forethought, self-reactiveness, and self-reflectiveness—is particularly challenging for women during this career stage. This phenomenon may contribute to the proverbial "broken rung," the step on the corporate ladder that slows the trajectory of many mid-career women.

This chapter addresses the false narratives, energy drains, and perfectionism that consume many mid-career women. You are given permission and encouragement to take charge by letting go of guilt, owning choices, setting boundaries, building positive energy, allowing and asking for help, and seeing yourself as a priority.

A significant portion of this chapter is focused on getting your "house in order," putting priorities in place so that you can make time and space for your *Now, Near, Next.* So, congratulations! By picking up this book and investing this time, you have already begun to activate your personal agency. Now the first challenge begins.

Embrace Grace over Guilt

You do not just feel bad about letting your kids, team, or boss down; you also feel guilty about practicing self-care, remorse for not helping aging parents enough, or embarrassment about telling a friend how stressed out you are—as if you do not have a right to feel this way.

—AMY WESTERVELT, 2018

In her book *Forget "Having It All,"* Amy Westervelt sums up perfectly what I believe most mid-career women feel regularly. And even as an empty-nester, it resonates with me. In fact, I found embarking on writing this book to be filled with irony. While attempting to author a guide to setting priorities and intentional career planning, I struggled to carve out time that would not detract from other commitments or responsibilities.

In the throes of a demanding career, it seemed selfish and almost deceitful to give time to authoring a book. I had a pattern of getting up at 5:00 a.m. and spending the early morning hours clearing email, working on projects, and attending to various task assignments that had built up the day before. My workday began at 5:00 a.m. and ended at 6:00 p.m. Working on evenings and weekends was also common. The demand for the job was great, but the time invested was not the fault of my employer. It was the lack of boundaries that I established.

I could not dedicate time to writing during the day and was too tired in the evening. However, the idea of refocusing those early morning hours on developing this book rather than beginning my workday filled me with guilt and concern that my employer would question my loyalty. I started writing each morning at 4:00 a.m. to accommodate my sense of justice.

Despite overcompensating to ensure that my integrity was unquestioned and my career uncompromised, I battled an internal struggle of guilt and exhaustion. It suddenly occurred to me that the same theme this book intends to address head-on was the very trap I found myself in. Not only did I need to give myself unapologetic time to invest in my growth and potential, but I also needed to give myself grace and put our *Now, Near, Next* framework into practice.

This poignant reminder is where we begin. Before considering proper self-care and investment in your growth, it is essential to:

- Make peace with your choices
- Establish healthy boundaries

Make Peace with Your Choices

I thought my early career had to be like a Venn diagram with my personal and professional life. Then I did not feel like I was giving enough to my kids or going above and beyond in my job. I would always feel guilty. I wish I had told myself there are only twenty-four hours in one day. It is OK for things to be bent diagrams.

—LINDSAY HASTINGS, PhD, professor

When my firstborn, Jordyn, was nine months old, my business travel ensued. On that first trip away, I recall calling my mother and crying. I felt terrible for leaving my little girl. With all her wisdom, my mom said, "I think you should run a hot bubble bath, order room service and a glass of wine, and enjoy the evening of peace. Whether you sulk or pamper yourself, you will still be gone. Use this time to take care of yourself. Make the most of this time away." That alone was comforting. And then she said, "And you are modeling choice for your daughter. She can choose to stay home or choose to work outside the home. You are showing her what is possible." Mic-drop moment!

According to *Fast Company*, 78% of mothers feel guilty for not spending enough time with their kids. At the same time, 42 percent of women reported feeling guilty about leaving work early for family obligations, compared to 29 percent of men, according to research conducted by the employee benefits provider Unum. Women feel guilty when working and guilty when parenting. Sneaking out early to pick up kids and then half listening about their day while attending to email perpetuates an endless pit in your stomach.

Guilt, however, is indiscriminate. Women who do not have children are not immune to feelings of guilt. A 2020 study by the

National Alliance for Caregiving (NAC) and AARP reported that "more than one in five Americans are caring for an aging parent, 61 percent of whom are women. Among those providing care, 61 percent work outside the home, and at least 45 percent have endured at least one financial impact." The complexities associated with aging, increased demand for time and attention, and the myriad of "shoulds" that we burden ourselves with add to feelings of guilt.

According to a study published in the *Journal of Personality and Social Psychology*, women reported higher levels of guilt than men even when controlling for other factors such as self-esteem and interpersonal conflict. These feelings lead to endless apologies and self-doubt: Sorry I'm late, sorry I didn't get your gym clothes washed, and sorry I need to take this call. The reality is that you are not falling short. You have made choices in the best interest of yourself and those that count on you. You are doing the best you can.

Zeigler (2020) suggests that instead of "I feel bad," consider "I made that choice because." In making peace with your choices, you must give yourself the grace to recognize when the benefits outweigh the drawbacks. If your choices are no longer consistent with your values or delivering positive outcomes, you can choose to change direction.

As Kimberly Rath puts it so eloquently, "I traveled 150 nights a year with over 2.5 million miles on United. All United gave me was two inches on my hips. I missed a lot of special days. But I always had cookies or balloons delivered for the occasion and turned birthdays and holidays into weekend experiences instead of two-hour events."

There are times when we must extend this same grace within our personal lives. How often do we run ragged to attend numerous family gatherings over the holidays or feel guilty when business travel overlaps with a birthday or an anniversary? What if we approached holidays and special celebrations as an event instead of a day? While it is natural to want to celebrate a birthday on the actual date, it can occur any day of the week when it is represented as an event rather than a day. Setting this expectation early for working parents, newlyweds, or empty-nesters can eliminate the tremendous pressure we put on ourselves.

Life is cumulative. It is not about what we missed but when we were present. Embracing grace means that we must be flexible, flow with the puts and takes, make peace with our choices, and be content with the totality of our investment in others and ourselves.

I remember I had to travel out of town and was going to miss my son's band concert. He had a solo. So, I was on the phone with my husband, and he was literally holding the phone so that I could hear. I also remember when the solo was over, I said, "'OK, I'm good." My husband said, "'Oh, no, you think you can hang up? You're going to be here for the whole thing. I'm here for the whole thing, so are you!" We just tried to make it work the best we could.

—MELINDA LEBOFSKY, CHRO

Activating your personal agency begins with taking ownership of your choices and circumstances. Guilt has its place and is a very human emotion. If you have genuinely hurt someone or behaved in a way inconsistent with your values, feeling guilt or regret is appropriate and should be addressed. However, if you are consumed with not doing enough or being enough, you do not have the energy to focus on what is *Next.* Letting go of guilt and regret is imperative in moving forward.

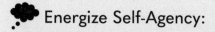

Energize Self-Agency:

In what specific situation can you give yourself grace by reframing your mental model from "I feel guilty about" to "I made this choice so that"?

Establish Healthy Boundaries

Love yourself enough to be fierce with your boundaries and your standards.

—ANN ELIZABETH MOHART, MD

When I first became a grandmother, affectionately referred to as CeCe, and Jordyn was a young mother, I was always eager to offer help, advice, and financial support. Occasionally, I found myself feeling taken advantage of or not appreciated. When sharing this with a dear friend, she questioned my intent and my daughter's receptivity. She wondered if I was leaning in for my self-interest and, in doing so, had implied to my daughter that I didn't think she could handle things on her own. *Hmm.*

Having the desire to help another person is a beautiful expression of empathy. However, setting boundaries without guilt is a significant, life-giving gift we can and should provide for ourselves. We can love and listen and empathize without jumping into the pool.

As a mom, sister, friend, daughter, and professional woman, it can be difficult not to immediately want to dive in and solve our loved ones' or colleagues' problems. However, people do not always want or need us to save the day, and in a professional setting, failing to set healthy boundaries may negatively impact your professional brand.

Professional Boundaries

For many years I was the only woman on the executive team. I am, by nature, helpful and hospitable. My male peers and I were often asked to speak at leadership events. Each of us had essentially the same title, brought a unique area of expertise, and had the support of our respective administrative assistants. Bottom line, we were each equally equipped and qualified to develop and prepare for a presentation.

However, leaning into my bias for action, I would take the responsibility of scheduling the meetings to gather us together, facilitate the discussion, take notes, and draft the PowerPoint deck. They would happily sit back, exercising little effort beyond opinions. In my mind, I was being helpful, and most important, I knew that the work would get done.

My mindset changed considerably one day when, just before we took the stage, all three men asked me questions. What am I supposed to cover? Who do I follow? As I was passing out my copy of the slide notes, I remember seeing another senior female leader who reported to me that she had observed this exchange and felt embarrassed. The "guys" would not have expected this catering from a male peer. In fact, they would not have expected that level of support from some of the women junior to me.

I realized then that I had enabled this dependency, created this expectation, and made it my professional brand—not exactly the brand I was going for. I didn't desire to be their caretaker, assistant, or handler. I was their professional equal, thought partner, and collaborator. We will cover professional brands in greater detail in chapter three.

From that day forward, I intentionally changed the way I approached these situations, setting clear boundaries about the role I was willing to take on. There is a difference between playing to strength to divide and conquer the work and taking on all of the jobs that others don't want to do. It wasn't easy to change my approach, and there was a fair number of attempts to appeal to my compassion or trigger guilt. However, I realized that I was enabling inequitable behavior and minimizing my professional contribution by taking on all the tasks and sharing equally in the outcome.

A study published with the American Psychological Association found that employees who set clear boundaries between work and non-work activities experienced less work-family conflict and reported higher levels of job satisfaction. Ironic that the very thing that could improve our mental, physical, and emotional health is the tool that we feel anxious to adopt.

Think of a boundary as a protective shield. This positive energy source serves as a force that surrounds your physical, mental, emotional, and spiritual well-being; an energy source that guards your time, relationships, and personal space. It is not a barrier or a wall but a dynamic, empowering, sanity-saving continuum. Depending on the context, here are some additional general guidelines that can help:

Clearly define your boundaries: Start by identifying areas or aspects of your life you want to set barriers around. It could be your personal time, work-life balance, relationships, or any other important aspect.

Understand your needs and values: Reflect on your personal needs and values. Consider what is profoundly important to you and what aligns with your long-term goals and well-being. This self-awareness will help you determine where you need to set boundaries.

Communicate your boundaries: Once you have identified your boundaries, communicate them effectively to the relevant people in your life. Clearly express your limits, expectations, and reasons for your boundaries. This can help prevent misunderstandings and conflicts.

Be assertive: It's essential to assertively uphold your boundaries. Learn to say "no" when necessary and express your needs and limits without feeling guilty or apologizing excessively. Remember that setting boundaries is about taking care of yourself and your well-being.

Practice self-care: Prioritize self-care to maintain physical, mental, and emotional well-being. This might include setting aside regular time for rest, relaxation, hobbies, and activities that bring you joy and fulfillment. You'll be better equipped to maintain boundaries by taking care of yourself.

Assess and adjust as needed: Regularly assess how well your boundaries work for you. Evaluate whether they are helping you achieve your goals and maintain a healthy balance. Adjust and refine your boundaries to ensure that they remain appropriate and effective.

Remember that setting boundaries is personal, and finding the right balance may take time. Forgive yourself, let go of guilt, and embrace a new beginning. Be patient with yourself and understand that it's a continuous journey of self-discovery and self-care.

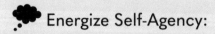 **Energize Self-Agency:**

What one area of your life do you need to protect with a boundary, a force field of positive energy?

Setting boundaries may feel selfish. However, setting limits does not mean that you focus only on that which is self-serving. It means focusing on that which is self-actualizing. You are not carving out time to the detriment of others, but rather, so that you can be the best version of yourself where it matters most.

Lending Time, Talent, or Treasure

How often do you find yourself overcommitted and regretting having said yes? Many of us were raised to be accommodating, helpful, and selfless. It is not that we cannot say no or do not have the backbone to create boundaries. We often genuinely want to participate in community-event planning, a school fundraiser, an extra project at work, and volunteering at church. What is our motivation for saying yes, and how does our involvement fit into our overall plan?

A study by Torstveit, Sutterlin, and Lugo (2016) revealed the correlation between guilt-proneness and empathy as well as guilt-proneness and helping behavior. For women, compassion proves to be a significant driver of the need to help. When coupled with guilt, there is an overwhelming desire to lean in.

Women are taught to be ultimately "other-centered." Research suggests that societal expectations and gender roles reinforce women's "other-centered" socialization. From an early age, girls are often socialized to prioritize others' needs and emotions over their own. They are encouraged to be nurturing, empathetic, and caring toward others, which can lead to developing a solely selfless identity.

Finding alternative ways to contribute can be helpful when you want to do something but are stretched. Is it time, talent, or treasure that the commitment demands? What can you give most freely of in that moment or future?

At various mid-career stages, I was too busy with work to volunteer in our children's schools (time). However, I could contribute financially to the fundraiser (treasure). Other times, money was tight, and work was demanding. In those instances, I volunteered to make phone calls or handle tasks I could do from my home or office (talent).

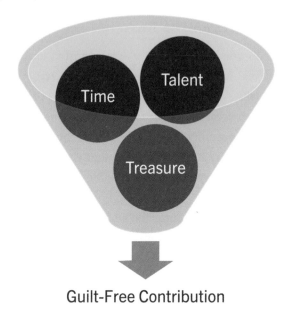

Guilt-Free Contribution

Saying no and creating limits may be time-bound (not now) or type-bound (time, talent, or treasure). Moreover, there are times to say no; as much as you want to help, you are overextended.

Authoring this book has challenged me to practice what it preaches. Embracing grace over guilt started with getting up at 4:00 a.m. to write until 5:00 a.m. However, I realized that I needed to establish boundaries. As a result, I took back my mornings and weekends for writing. Beyond urgent issues, my employer still gets my undivided attention from 7:00 a.m. to 7:00 p.m., Monday through Friday.

In terms of owning my choices, I gave this project voice. Rather than minimizing or watering down my *Next* out of fear that my loyalty would be questioned, I made my effort and plans public. Letting myself invest in my talent and passion felt liberating and empowering. Yet this transparency also came with some uncomfortable moments, judgment, and skepticism by some. More on that later. It also created an unexpected sense of accountability, which isn't a bad thing. Ultimately, recognize that you don't have to do everything alone. Delegate tasks and responsibilities when possible, in both personal and professional settings. Asking for help when needed can prevent getting overwhelmed and enable you to maintain your boundaries. Believe it or not, other people want to help and are sometimes a better solution than we think!

Ask for Help

We expect women to work like they do not have children and raise children as if they do not work.

—AMY WESTERVELT

According to a report by the United Nations, women perform 2.6 times the unpaid care and domestic work than men do, including cooking, cleaning, and caring for children and elderly family members. Looking back to 2000, the workforce had more women with advanced degrees working outside the home, earning more money, and working longer hours while raising children than in the preceding decades. As such, today's mid-career women were likely raised by mothers who "could do it all" or were role-modeling that superwoman prowess.

I was raised by one of those incredible women who appeared to balance a marriage, business, household, and raising my sister and me. It appeared there was nothing she could not do. My aspirations early on were to emulate that example. She made it look easy, giving me no doubt that I could have and do it all—it wasn't until adulthood that I understood the challenges she faced and sacrifices she made. However, those early years were formative, and as such, the generational expectations of being a successful working mother or caregiver continued and were role-modeled for my daughter.

Today, women account for 47 percent of the labor force, and 40.5 percent are the primary or co-breadwinners for their families (U.S. Bureau of Labor Statistics, 2022). However, women spend 37 percent more time than men do on household chores and caregiving (2018). Women continue to take on the more significant burden of child-rearing, elder care, emotional support, health-care decisions, etc.

So while there is a greater gender balance in the workforce today, societal expectations have remained relatively unchanged for over fifty years. Women are often expected to juggle multiple responsibilities, including work and family. They often feel pressure to appear competent and independent and may worry that asking for help at home could undermine these perceptions. At the same time, asking for help at work could lead to negative perceptions or judgments from coworkers, supervisors, or peers that they cannot effectively manage their personal and professional lives.

Jordyn works in the home raising her three children, two under three years old, and balances several creative side businesses. Even when she is stretched and trying to manage everything, I have witnessed her refusal to ask for or allow help, even from her very willing husband. Not only does she seem compelled to prove that the female superpower has been genetically continued, but she assumes greater responsibility for independently doing it all as the one who stays home. Any attempt to assist with laundry, housework, or meal preparation is met with resistance and defensiveness, as though she is being judged.

Women working outside the home often compensate for their time away from the family by doing more household chores. In doing so, these activities become high-stakes, emotionally. Not washing the soccer uniform or forgetting to pick up a gallon of milk feels like a personal failure. Allowing support, even when offered, leads to feelings of inadequacy.

When I read the example above to Jordyn, she smiled in agreement. She bears a deep belief that somehow, accepting help represents failure. Her impression is that I single-handedly, successfully managed our household while working full-time— and the social cycle continues. The truth is, I struggled; I made personal sacrifices; I felt deep guilt, but I did the best I could. This juxtaposition between her memory and my reality became a teaching and bonding moment for both of us. I shattered the illusion of being a superwoman, humbly confessing the challenges and toll of trying to do it all, just as my mom has shared with me.

What a gift it would be to the young women in our lives if we modeled asking for help, inviting support, and doing so with strength and confidence.

Energize Self-Agency:

How often do you reject help because of a false narrative?

Key learning from our qualitative research is the value of asking for help. Although women are often not naturally good at giving up control or letting someone else take on the burden, doing so may be the most liberating thing we can do. There may be someone who could complete the task better and faster and would feel immense joy in helping. However, women must overcome the feeling of failure if they are not single-handedly doing it all!

It's that cycle. The logical weight of that responsibility and knowing that at the end of the day, it would always fall on me first and foremost, and I didn't want it any other way, but that was not something I could ever escape. And then I always had the responsibility at work. And so, there were times when I thought the balance of my life was out of control, and multiple times I remember coming home and thinking, I cannot do this anymore. This is not sustainable. And I felt like there was just nothing left of me. And what saved me was being very humble and open to accepting help and acknowledging there is no glory in being a superwoman and doing everything; you have to accept help.

—ANN ELIZABETH MOHART, MD

Asking for and receiving help is not a sign of weakness; it is a sign of leadership. The research suggests that asking for help can be a powerful tool for problem-solving, learning, and improving self-esteem. It is important to remember that asking for help is a sign of strength and willingness to learn and grow. Asking for help can become a superpower and is beneficial in so many ways. Here are some reasons why asking for help can be a promising idea:

Save time and energy: Sometimes we have too much to do. When you ask for help, you can get the assistance you need more quickly. You save time and conserve positive energy.

Overcome obstacles: We inevitably encounter challenges at work or home. Asking for help can provide us with the support and resources we need.

Building relationships: Asking for help can be an excellent way to build relationships with others. When someone helps you, it creates a sense of connection and gratitude that can strengthen your relationship.

Gain new knowledge or skills: By asking for help, you can learn from someone who has more experience or knowledge than you have. This can help you develop new skills and knowledge.

Gain a new perspective: Asking for help can give you innovative ideas and approaches.

Pulling on the "time, talent, and treasure" concept, you can ask for and receive help in exchange for returning the favor, bartering a skill, or contributing monetarily. Furthermore, receiving support when you have nothing to return is also OK. One of the greatest blessings you can offer another person is help without an exchange.

The reality is that women can be capable and resourceful simultaneously. Balancing career, family, and other demands throughout your career requires embracing help. Applying the same executive prowess of delegation, negotiation, and bartering to your personal life is liberating and worth celebrating.

If we approach our personal lives with the same shared responsibility that we do our professional lives, we will succeed mightily. Every successful leader understands the value of surrounding themselves with talent and building a stronger team. Why would we employ a different construct at home or within our community?

Delegating some of the responsibilities does not mean you have to give up those things that fill your cup. When inventorying your many competing demands, take a moment to consider those things that bring you joy, not just the things that diminish your guilt. If you love to cook, do not delegate that responsibility. If you enjoy grocery shopping, keep that task for yourself. However, thoughtfully consider how you enlist the help and support of other members of your family unit. Someone could prepare the salad, bring in and put away the groceries, clean the dishes, or take your mother to a doctor appointment.

For seventeen years, I made sack lunches every day for my two children. Both preferred to bring their lunch to school. As a working mom, there were many times when I needed help to actively participate in school activities. However, every day, my kids went to school with a lunch I lovingly packed, often with a little handwritten note inside. When they were in high school, friends would question why I didn't have the kids make their own lunches. It wasn't that they couldn't; it was that I found motherhood in that task, and it wasn't something I wanted to give up.

Until we have cleared the table with the commitments and responsibilities that consume us in our personal lives, we can't fully make room for intentional career investment.

 Energize Self-Agency:

When you inventory the significant responsibility of household chores, caregiving, and emotional support, what one thing could you delegate starting immediately?

An important note: When enlisting the help of others, you may have to let go of some perfectionist tendencies. Clothes may be put away differently than you would prefer, groceries may not be as organized, and the dishwasher may not be perfectly stacked. Part of asking for and receiving help is letting others do it their way and being OK with that.

This is a very difficult concept for me. I am very particular, to a fault. However, I try to keep in mind that if it gets done, who cares? What if good enough was enough? So, with an abundance of resistance, I do not reload the dishwasher, reorganize the pantry, or refold the laundry when others lean in to help. Trust me; it certainly improves relationships with the person who has offered their assistance.

Asking for help allows you to channel your energy and momentum toward the things in your life with higher value and priority. Here are a few tips to consider when making the ask:

- Provide context or explain why you need assistance, which can make your request more compelling. It helps the other person understand the importance or urgency of your request.
- Identify the person who is most likely to be able to help you with your specific request. Consider their expertise, availability, and willingness to assist.
- Clearly communicate what you need assistance with. State your request concisely and precisely so the person understands exactly what you're asking for, e.g., I need you to empty the dishwasher each time it is clean and take out the trash on Mondays.
- Once someone has helped you, follow up and express your gratitude. Let them know the outcome or how their assistance made a positive impact.

Generate Positive Energy

Nothing is worth more than laughter. It is strength to laugh and to abandon oneself, to be light.

—FRIDA KAHLO, Mexican painter

In physics, kinetic energy is generated when an object is forced from a resting position into motion. The kinetic energy gained during acceleration is maintained unless the thing's speed changes. Kinetic energy is absolute, either optimistic and moving or zero and still. This metaphor of forward motion and creating sustainable energy around your mid-career will be referenced throughout this book.

When you have released guilt and formalized boundaries, you can assume a healthy resting position. To further take charge of your self-agency, you must channel your energy and the energy around you to force your mid-career into motion and create continuous momentum. Energy is both intrinsic and extrinsic.

Talent Plus,® a behavioral science company that annually studies the talents of millions of individuals around the globe, has found that the theme of "positivity" is a core natural talent among the most successful people studied. It is a universal theme and highly predicts job performance and success in one's professional role. Using kinetic energy as a metaphor for bringing velocity to your career path, positivity can propel you into motion and accelerate you forward.

Those who positively see the world are more likely to:

- Feel motivated and energized
- Be less affected by stress
- Build better relationships with coworkers, clients, and leaders

A positive attitude can help boost your self-confidence, which can be beneficial when taking on new challenges, speaking up in meetings, or asking for a raise or promotion, all of which you will be challenged to do throughout this book. Additionally, we know from decades of research that positivity is linked to a longer life span, less stress, reduced health risks, and increased overall well-being.

When you approach challenges and obstacles with a positive mindset, you are more likely to develop creative solutions to problems. In addition to practicing positive self-talk, which we will cover deeply in chapter seven, here are other ways to generate positive energy:

Practice gratitude: Focusing on the positive aspects of your life can help counteract negative thoughts and emotions. Writing in a gratitude journal each morning or before bed provides a structured approach to taking time each day to reflect on what you are thankful for. Refrain from holding out for perfect circumstances when considering what you are grateful for. Some days, hot coffee, a pet's cuddle, or the smell of cut grass may be worthy of appreciation.

Practice self-care: Taking care of your physical and mental health can help reduce negativity. Make time for activities that bring you joy and relaxation, such as exercise, meditation, or spending time in nature. Depending on your life's circumstances, this may mean enjoying a cup of coffee before the children wake up or soaking in a hot bubble bath before bed. Find the time that works in your schedule and put boundaries around it. Sacrificing self-care not only impacts your physical wellness but also leads to resentment and emotional distress. We will loop back to this in chapter nine.

Surround yourself with positivity: Energy is both intrinsic and extrinsic. Creating, sustaining, and surrounding yourself with positive energy starts with eliminating negativity from your life, beginning with identifying the sources of negativity. In addition to eliminating time with negative people, spend time with people who lift you and make you feel good about yourself.

I had a girlfriend tell me years ago that she had decided not to hang out with people who did not make her laugh. Fortunately for me, I made the cut. While she was moderately joking, her point was that life is short and time is precious. Spending discretionary time with people who give rather than deplete energy is worth consideration.

Why is it important to minimize if not eliminate the time you spend with negative people? Firstly, negative people can influence your attitude and outlook. Research indicates that behavior breeds behavior. After lunch with a friend who sees the world through an empty glass, cannot find the silver lining in anything, and sits in a victim mentality, you may feel drained.

Spending too much time with negative people can alter your mood and positivity and challenge your thinking, bringing greater scrutiny and skepticism about your life. As important, negative people are more often discouraging. These individuals will not encourage you to shoot for the stars, follow your dreams, and invest unapologetically in yourself. This limiting feedback can hold you back and further reinforce negative self-talk. You don't need dream crushers in your life.

🗯️ Energize Self-Agency:

How can you minimize time spent with negative people who may influence your attitude, mood, and positivity?

Look at the people, situations, and environments that tend to bring negativity into your life. Once you identify these sources, you can minimize your exposure to them. Remember, eliminating negativity from your life is a process that takes time and effort. Be patient and kind to yourself as you work toward a more positive outlook. Seek positive influences in your life through books, podcasts, or other sources that fill your heart and soul with sources of energy.

Back to boundaries: Of course, there are those family members, coworkers, or neighbors that you may be unable to avoid altogether. You know the ones. You get that tense feeling in your chest when you see them or sigh when their number appears on your phone. You can have grace and boundaries.

- Choose your battles: Not every disagreement or issue needs to be addressed. Consider the importance of the matter and decide whether it's worth engaging in a conflict or if it's better to let certain things go. Sometimes, accepting differences and maintaining a peaceful coexistence can be the best approach.
- Respond, don't react: Instead of reacting impulsively to provocative or hurtful comments, take a moment to compose yourself and respond thoughtfully.
- Focus on common ground: Look for areas of agreement or shared values to build upon. Find topics or activities you can enjoy together and focus on nurturing those aspects of your relationship.
- Set limits: Commit your time and attention while maintaining a healthy boundary. Stop by for dessert rather than staying for dinner.

Practice mindfulness: Besides minimizing external sources of negative energy, be attentive to activating positivity within you. A few years ago, I was struggling to fall asleep at night. Not only was I going through the breakup of a very toxic relationship and pursing my doctorate, but work was also emotionally taxing. I recalled that when my grandson would stay the night, we would play lullaby music as a soothing way to sleep. I began a ritual, setting a forty-five-minute timer and playing this same music every evening as I went to bed. I soon learned that "Puff the Magic Dragon" was not terribly calming, so I switched to meditation music, which I still play every evening.

Filling your mind, body, and soul with positive intention can generate a greater sense of self-actualized calm and confidence.

 Energize Self-Agency:

What is one way that you can generate more positive energy in your life?

Conclusion

Women are responsible for most of their family's mental, physical, and emotional care, create few boundaries, and feel more guilt than men, leaving their agency to others. We have addressed the false narratives, energy drains, and perfectionism that consume many mid-career women. We have challenged the idea that the only options are selfless or selfish, always putting others' needs first or focusing only on self-interest. Instead, we suggest that women engage in honest self-discovery to recognize where they are *Now* and become their best selves, personally and professionally.

Letting go and taking charge will help you feel more engaged, motivated, and fulfilled in your career. Remember that taking control of your agency is a journey, and taking things one step at a time is OK. Be patient with yourself and celebrate your progress along the way. With a foundation of empowerment, you are ready to move to chapter two, where you will proclaim your purpose by declaring your professional mission, vision, and values.

Reflection: Take Charge

The miles we earn on guilt trips...

— **SOMYA MATHUR,** Senior Director, Diversity, Equity, and Inclusion

Somya Mathur is a social psychologist by education and considers herself a lifelong student of human behavior. It is particularly fascinating for her to help companies create an exceptional employee culture by leveraging data-driven insights and actions. Over the last decade and a half, she has lived and worked in India, the UK, and Germany and now resides in America. Currently, she works as a DEI leader at a global animal health-care company where she is leading an important agenda of creating a more equitable and fair work environment where people can do their best work. She has a master's degree in social psychology from the London School of Economics, UK, and continues to remain associated through the alumni networks. She has previously worked with consulting giants like Deloitte, IBM, and Aon Hewitt. In her personal time, Somya loves traveling, photography, continuing her sommelier education, and learning the piano with her husband, Nick, and daughter, Niya.

The year was 2016, and in the last six months, two incidents had taken place at work. It was about 5:00 p.m. on a Wednesday when I attempted to wrap up my work with some frenetic energy and a degree of desperation. Delhi traffic is a mess, and my ten-month-old daughter's school was at the other end of a bottleneck in the road. My manager came up behind me to say, "Leaving at 5:00, Somya? Half day today?"

Before that, I had found myself in a similar predicament when working late at night for a prominent client in Asia. A senior partner saw me and registered the time on the clock. "Eight p.m.? Shouldn't you be at home with your baby, Somya?"

Very early in motherhood, I realized that I could do no right. I was either negligent or indulgent. I was either maniacal about my career or not ambitious enough. The productivity and quality of my output, even feedback from my clients, were all second to the grade I received as a new mom from leaders who knew very little about my family. I had fallen prey to such generalizations all my life. Sometimes in London as an "Indian student," sometimes in India as a "London-returned Indian." These labels seemed to have been plucked from thin air and gifted to me quite liberally—a new mom, expecting mom, working mom, traditional mom, modern mom, and even good mom or bad mom, depending on who was speaking.

It was increasingly obvious to me at twenty-nine years old that labels are easy to get but hard to get rid of. If we hold a tiny glass of water for a minute, we can bear it, but if we have it all day, every day, for a month or a year, it can quickly become onerous. Despite seeing role models who seemingly managed work and their families brilliantly, women are often put through the "doubt chamber" until this doubt stemming from others starts to be internalized as self-doubt. We begin to wonder if, indeed, our priorities have changed unrecognizably. We tend to question our ambition and our ability to juggle responsibilities. We are often led down the path of asking if our lives are imbalanced because of our choices. I saw other new mothers battling the same psychological syndrome. When I took a broader, more comprehensive approach and started listening to others, it was clear that I was not alone.

One night, sitting with my mother, I confided in her about the thoughts that were crossing my mind—that, just maybe, I was not cut out for this. Her words were simple and effective, as always. She made me extrapolate my life to three years later, when my daughter would be in school all day, and ask myself, *What will I do at home?* She asked me if it was worth second-guessing myself for something I went to school for, had led to jobs with tremendous career potential, and I already had a track record of success. Would it not be better to keep working through these years instead of reentering an entirely new workforce, years later, that I no longer understood? My husband, too, opted to stay home with our daughter for a year because his role had more flexibility, and he wanted to offer me as much support as possible to stay in the workforce. He quickly joined my mother to ensure that I felt supported through significant transitions such as my first business trip after becoming a mother.

Today, as my daughter turns seven, I lead DEI for a global company of 5,500 people. Looking back, just the act of confiding in someone and asking for help stands out to me as a life-changing move. The years went by anyway, and my daughter is now starting second grade. Often, I drop her off at school and recall my mother's question: "What will you do all day when she is at school?"

It did not matter if someone thought I should be at home with my daughter or if I was clocking in a half day after working for eight hours. It did not matter if people thought I was a good or a bad mother. The only approval I needed was from myself and my daughter, who proudly dreams big in part because she sees her mother achieve her dreams consistently. I now know for a fact that strong women raise strong women, and there is an indelible, incredible strength in numbers. So even if you do not need to, I urge women to work and carve their own space and identity. When there are many of us, people will think twice before pointing fingers at any of us. I implore you to hold on to your courage of conviction, and even when doubt exists all around you, remember that it does not have to permeate.

CHAPTER TWO

Proclaim Your Purpose

You can make more money; you can't make more life.

— **LINDA K. BAX,** my mom

MALALA YOUSAFZAI, A PAKISTANI ACTIVIST FOR GIRLS' EDUCATION AND THE YOUNGEST NOBEL PRIZE LAUREATE, had a clear sense of mission to fight for the education and empowerment of girls and women. Her vision was of a world where all girls could receive an education and fulfill their potential, and her values of courage, determination, and resilience guided her actions. Yousafzai's sense of social responsibility was bold, global, and altruistic. Her sense of purpose was clear.

While you may not be taking on social justice, we all have the opportunity and platform to proclaim our purpose. Reflecting and developing a personal mission, vision, and values statement helps you clarify your intention, direction, and nonnegotiable values. It enables you to identify what matters most, what you want to achieve, and how you want to live. With a defined mission, vision, and list of core values, you can concentrate your energy and efforts on what is most important to you, prioritize your activities, and eliminate distractions, making it easier to achieve your goals.

Chapter two invites you to take inventory of your current situation, envision what could be, set your aspirations for the future, and commit to being the lead architect of your path forward. Take time to be introspective and reflective. For some, this chapter will feel intuitive and inspiring. For others, the exercise may feel challenging or thought-provoking. Wherever you land, live into this moment so that you may confidently proclaim your purpose!

Declare Core Values

Every time I have gone against either what I wanted to do or what my true opinion was, I've always suffered in my ability to work and my ability to deliver and succeed.

—Ayesha Khanna, PhD, Cofounder and CEO, Addo

A few times early in my career, I found myself working in an environment that was dysfunctional or toxic. While I have worked with many excellent leaders over the years, there were some I would characterize as insecure, narcissistic, or downright mean. I recall telling a senior leader early in my career, "I feel like I am prostituting myself, staying in this position purely for the salary while putting up with emotionally abusive behavior." Working in environments that challenged my core principles consumed valuable energy, took a mental and physical toll, and in every case prompted my *Next!*

In a study published in the journal *Psychological Science*, researchers found that people who pursued extrinsic goals such as money and fame were less likely to experience positive emotions and more likely to experience negative emotions than those who sought intrinsic goals such as personal growth and close relationships. Before declaring a path to your *Next*, you must reflect on what you value most and what you are unwilling to compromise.

If you're taking time away from your family or taking time away from the things that you love, it better be worth it.

—Amanda Fedje, business owner

Values give life to your brand. As such, your nonnegotiables do not have to be limited to what is illegal, immoral, or makes someone's mama mad, as my mom would say. Being true to your core values will be critical to finding purpose in each professional career stage. Internal conflict eats away happiness and ignites guilt when values are compromised for title, money, or position.

Think of any company recognized for excellence in its industry; each has documented its core values. These principles set the standard for behavioral conduct, decision-making, judgment, and priorities. When companies publicly express their core values, they send a message to the world that they are committed to, and therefore should be held accountable for, living out these principles.

As professional women, we, too, should name our core values. Like organizations, core values anchor who you are, what you stand for, and how you approach life. To clarify what uniquely distinguishes you, it is crucial to begin with what you cherish, hold dear, and keep sacred.

As you consider proclaiming your purpose, you are encouraged to take three steps: name your core values, share them with others, and check in periodically.

Naming Core Values: Putting words on paper allows you to create personal commitment and accountability. It is essential to write down the four to six values that are most core to who you are and what you stand for, creating a visual reminder to reference when deciding or navigating a challenge.

Dignity, Authenticity, Positivity, Integrity, Passion — **Cynthia**

Integrity, Kindness, Positivity, Love, Belonging — **Kimberly**

Make your values known: When you put your nonnegotiables into the universe, you empower your agency. One way to publish your core values is to include them on your bio, résumé/CV, LinkedIn profile, etc.

Energizing Your
Now, Near, Next

Cynthia Bentzen-Mercer, PhD

(She/Her)

Strategic Executive, Sociologist, Servant Leader, Speaker, Author, Board Certified Coach / Core Values: Passion, Positivity, Authenticity, Integrity, Excellence

Listing your values tells the world what you care about. Doing so invites the world to know who you are and what you stand for. Writing down and sharing your core values can guide ethical and moral decisions and ensure your actions are consistent with your principles.

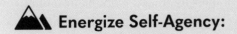

Energize Self-Agency:

Identify your core values.

Check in periodically: Recognizing that our values may evolve, checking in with yourself regularly is essential. Throughout your emerging career, travel, working long hours, and around-the-clock availability may have energized your drive and ambition. However, in mid-career, you may be conflicted about the increased value you place on personal relationships and professional aspirations. It can be easy to grow both frustrated and resentful if we do not take the time to recognize and honor our evolving values.

When opportunities are presented, check in with your guiding principles. When you feel taken advantage of or overextended, check in with your core values. Naming, sharing, and revisiting your values occasionally helps to remind you of the *why* behind your choices, compromises, and sacrifices. You retain your agency when there is clarity about what matters most to you.

Develop Your Why

Chase after the dream; don't chase after the money.

— **Lisa Sterling,** Chief People Officer

Women often spend so much time getting through the hustle of the given moment that they fail to declare a mission and envision what is possible. A clear and inspiring mission statement can be a powerful source of motivation. It can help you stay committed to your goals even when facing obstacles or setbacks by reminding you of the bigger picture and why you are working toward it. Your mission statement is your *why*. Your values should inform your mission; they are the more profound explanation of why you have chosen your path.

Developing a personal mission statement requires self-reflection and introspection. It encourages you to explore your strengths, weaknesses, values, and aspirations, leading to greater self-awareness and self-knowledge.

An exercise that can be helpful is to consider what you get paid to do (or wish you were paid to do). Think of this not as the job description but as the true essence of your purpose. Focus not on the tactical parts of your job description but on the deeper *why*. Having a clear mission allows you to align your actions with your values and beliefs and serves as a guide for making ethical and moral decisions consistent with your broader purpose. Your mission statement should give meaning to your deeper why. Ask yourself:

> *What drives me, compels me, and gets me out of bed beyond a paycheck?*
>
> *How do I want to contribute to my community or society at large?*

Having worked with many organizations in their exploration to create a clear and concise mission statement, this takes time. If ideas do not immediately jump to your mind, that is OK. You may need to spend a few days reflecting on these questions. This may be your first time considering your mission beyond your organization. When ready, review your answers. What common themes or patterns emerge?

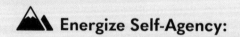 **Energize Self-Agency:**

Author your concise and compelling mission statement.

Your statement should be future-focused, aspirational, and action-oriented. It should align with your values and inspire you to act. Consider breaking your mission statement into three parts: why, who, and how. For example:

By empowering self-agency and challenging social and self-imposed limitations, I serve to equip every person with insight into their God-given talents so they may unleash and grow their full potential and live into their most profound sense of purpose.

— Cynthia Bentzen-Mercer

Why: unleash and develop their full potential and live into their most profound sense of purpose

Who: every person

How: by empowering self-agency and challenging social and self-imposed limitations

I passionately embrace my strengths to help people unlock limitless possibilities and experience exponential growth by discovering, developing, and celebrating the extraordinary potential within them.

— Kimberly, coauthor

Why: unlock limitless possibilities and experience exponential growth

Who: people

How: by discovering, developing, and celebrating the extraordinary potential that resides within them

A mission statement can help to define what success means to you, keep you focused on your goals, and remind you of why your work is essential and meaningful. Implement your mission statement by setting specific, measurable, and achievable goals that align with it. Celebrate your progress and use setbacks as opportunities for learning and growth.

One way to do this is by setting aside dedicated time each quarter to reflect on your mission and values and assess whether your current actions and decisions align with them. This could involve journaling, meditation, or talking with a trusted mentor or friend. Chapter five will explore the importance of mentorship and a support system.

Additionally, it is helpful to clearly understand what success looks like in terms of your career and personal life. This could involve setting specific, measurable goals for yourself such as achieving professional success or carving out more quality time with your family.

Developing a mission statement can help you live a more intentional, fulfilling life by providing a clear sense of purpose and direction. It can also help you make decisions aligned with your values and goals, leading to greater satisfaction in your personal and professional life.

Inspire Your Vision

Put your intention into what you love.

—Jenny Svoboda, entrepreneur

At what point did we narrow our path? Many of us represent the generation encouraged to speak up for ourselves, pursue our goals and aspirations, challenge gender stereotypes, and be anything we wanted to be! Remember that little girl who wanted to be a pilot, a news anchor, a president, a model, an actress, and a singer?

We would proclaim to whomever would listen precisely what we wanted to be when we grew up. We were bold, fearless, and—for me, with an average singing voice—unrealistic.

As we entered our careers as emerging professionals, we were focused, hungry, and ambitious. Opportunities were plentiful, and we had fewer competing demands. We were able to make sacrifices and exercise our self-agency. However, upon reaching mid-career, life gets more complex, advancement narrows, and many women begin the arduous daily grind. Our vision of what is possible becomes overshadowed by our *Now*.

Great organizations have ambitious and inspiring vision statements. These statements help us to understand *what* the company aspires to accomplish and *who* will benefit. Vision statements are often publicly shared to let the world know the bold contributions a company seeks to make. As professional women, we, too, should take the time to imagine what is possible.

Here are several ways the extraordinary women we spoke to visualize their aspirations:

Reflect on your passions: Take some time to reflect on what truly inspires and excites you. Consider your passions, talents, and values.

Set clear goals: Once you have identified your passions, set clear and specific goals that align with your vision.

Seek inspiration from others: Look for role models and mentors who have succeeded in areas like your vision. We will address this further in chapter five.

Expand knowledge and skills: Continuously learn and acquire new knowledge and skills related to your vision.

Develop a positive mindset: Cultivate a positive mindset and believe in your abilities.

To inspire and empower individuals to unleash their potentiality to achieve personal and professional collective joy, creating a better world.

— **Kimberly,** coauthor

A personal vision statement helps you gain clarity about your desired future. It enables you to envision what you want to achieve, how you want to live, and the impact you want to have. A personal vision statement should describe your long-term aspirations, goals, and values. The critical elements of a personal vision statement include:

Clarity: A personal vision statement should be clear and specific.

Inspiration: The statement should inspire and motivate, encouraging you to strive toward your goals.

Future-oriented: The vision statement should focus on the future, describing what you want to achieve and how you want to live your life rather than what you want to avoid or escape.

Values-driven: A personal vision statement should reflect your values, guiding your actions and decisions.

Measurable: The statement should include specific, quantifiable goals that you can work toward and track progress on.

To make a meaningful contribution to a society that embraces each person's unique gifts so that all would find dignity, joy, and purpose in their life's work.

— **Cynthia Bentzen-Mercer**

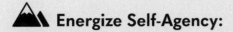 **Energize Self-Agency:**

Define your vision for the future.

A personal vision statement should provide a clear and inspiring direction for your life, guiding your decisions and actions toward your long-term goals and aspirations.

Conclusion

It is not uncommon for professional women to feel overwhelmed by the day-to-day demands of their jobs and family responsibilities, leaving little time to reflect on their long-term goals and aspirations. However, taking a step back and thinking about your values, mission, and vision is essential, as this can provide direction and purpose in your personal and professional life.

By taking the time to establish your mission and vision, you can better prioritize your time and energy, making sure that your daily actions align with your long-term goals and aspirations. Developing a personal mission, vision, and values statement can help you lead a more fulfilling and purposeful life by providing a clear direction, focus, and motivation to achieve your goals, live in alignment with your values, and positively impact the world. With a clear sense of direction, you are ready to look up and forward, reveal your natural talents, and assess your current state for current and future roles.

Reflection: Proclaim Your Purpose

The company was looking for a unicorn but expected them to behave like crocodiles.

— **Kristin Torres Mowat,** Partner, Health Velocity Capital

Kristin currently serves as a partner at Health Velocity Capital, a venture capital firm with over $500M assets under management investing in health-care innovators. She comes to investing with over fifteen years of operating experience in health-care software and services organizations, serving as a senior executive within a Fortune 200 health-care services company and helping to lead and scale a health-care software company from the early stages through IPO. Kristin previously served as SVP Corporate and Business Development for Castlight Health and was a senior executive at DaVita. Kristin has extensive experience serving on boards and leading health-care and technology companies through critical growth periods, fundraising, and M&A transactions. Kristin began her career at Bain & Co. and is from Mexico City. She received her BA, MBA, and JD from Stanford University. With her technology entrepreneur husband, she lives in California and raises two sons in a bilingual household.

It takes courage...to endure the sharp pains of self-discovery rather than choose to take the dull pain of unconsciousness that would last the rest of our lives.

— **Marianne Williamson,** American author

I remember when I fell in love with leadership. I was in high school, and our teacher, Mr. Barney, led us through a quarter course on the United Nations that culminated in the class taking over the school for two days and running a mock United Nations session with the participation of every single high school student, each representing a delegate. I was the Secretary General, opening and closing the General Assembly and welcoming our keynote speaker, then the *real* Secretary General, the Honorable Boutros Boutros-Ghali, to our school. Since then, I have intentionally studied others and worked on my own leadership.

I have sought to work at leading companies for people trusted and respected as leaders by the people they lead, in learning cultures and in roles where I would be challenged in my own leadership. I have used these as criteria in looking for and selecting professional opportunities. I have had the example, support, mentorship, and sponsorship of many generous and inspiring friends and colleagues along the way.

I learned what may seem obvious: our personal values and fundamental principles profoundly impact the kinds of leaders we are because they guide our actions and decision-making. Yet we often think about all the observed characteristics of leaders when thinking about what defines them: their presence, behaviors, communication style, etc. It has been my experience that the most challenging and impactful work I have done to become a better leader is to reflect and acknowledge my blind spots, iterate on my vision and values, and ask myself if I am living them or simply saying them—to acknowledge when I am being driven disproportionately by my self-interested ambition above my responsibility to serve my organization and others and to embrace vulnerability in front of others. These processes have been humbling and empowering all at once.

By clarifying my vision and values, I can set a more consistent example of aligning with them, which is fundamental to earning trust as a leader. I have revisited and refined my vision many times. However, it has consistently been about being a leader in the eyes of others, working to positively impact health care for people, contributing meaningfully to my family's finances and the broader economy, and prioritizing my health and well-being through fitness, nutrition, and prevention. Over time, I included as part of my vision (and dreams) to be a mother of two (which I gratefully am). My personal core values have not varied since I developed them: Service. Family. Accountability. Growth. Gratitude. Wellness.

Though these are clear to me and seem easy to live by in the best of times, it has been during challenging situations when they have served me best. A leader I admire and worked for told me on more than one occasion that I needed to show more aggression—"pound the table," "show them no mercy," and "don't be so collaborative," he said. And yet by every metric, I was delivering business results and growing people while contributing talent to the rest of the organization in my style.

I was initially frustrated by the feedback and felt unappreciated simply because I did not act like him and the rest of the team, who were primarily male. I expressed to my mentor that I felt as though he were looking for a unicorn on the team and wanted it to behave like a crocodile. I challenged myself to consider it and think what it would look like and take for me to act that way, and it just did not feel genuine or appeal to me to act that way. This tested my values and my vision. I am truly grateful for all the feedback he gave me repeatedly, because it forced me to pressure-test and intentionally work on continuously improving upon the kind of leader I aspire to be.

It is clear to me that I carry fire in my belly to achieve ambitious goals and deliver on what I believe is my responsibility to have a positive impact on the lives of others. I am also now clear that there is strength and power in *my* style of carrying myself and behaving. I, too, can have impact, visibility, and power while embracing analytical intellect, empathy, and emotional intelligence.

CHAPTER THREE

Reveal Your Zeal

Find out who you are and do it on purpose.

—**Dolly Parton,** American singer, songwriter, and actress

"ZEAL" IS DEFINED BY THE *MERRIAM-WEBSTER* DICTIONARY AS "a strong feeling of interest and enthusiasm that makes someone very eager or determined to do something." Synonyms include passion, gusto, vigor, energy, and zest. Revealing your zeal requires both authenticity and self-awareness. Authenticity starts with self-awareness—deeply understanding your values, strengths, weaknesses, and motivations. It involves recognizing and embracing your true self, including your unique qualities, experiences, and perspectives. To be authentic means to be true to yourself and genuine in your thoughts, actions, and expressions. It involves living in alignment with your values, beliefs, and personal identity rather than conforming to external expectations or societal pressures.

Being authentic is essential for living a fulfilling and meaningful life. It allows you to honor your true self, build genuine connections, inspire others, and make choices that align with your values. When you are true to yourself, you can explore your strengths and areas for improvement. This self-awareness fosters personal development and enables you to continuously evolve and grow.

With clarity of purpose, chapter three moves you to more profound self-discovery and an awakening of your potential. You are challenged to assess where you are relative to your mission, vision, and values, identify your God-given gifts and talents, and magnify the beautiful, unique person you are.

Look Up, Within, and Forward!

Choose a job you love and you'll never work a day in your life!

— **Confucius,** philosopher

For some, mid-career feels like a merry-go-round. You start in your emerging career eager to jump on. You pick the pink pony and hold on tight. You might move to the purple pony during the first stop. Look, Mom, no hands! However, a few years later, you look up and are still belted in the same saddle, on the same ride, following behind a new group of riders, going in circles. You need a bigger amusement park and a more challenging ride!

Feeling Stuck

Let's face it, mid-career covers much ground. While we don't explicitly use an age band, this is a twenty-plus-year time frame for many women. It is not uncommon to get married, have children, get divorced, complete postgraduate school, move, change jobs, become an empty-nester, support aging parents, and go through menopause, all during mid-career. At least, that's been my experience. While every woman's journey is unique, getting stuck somewhere along the way is common. In addition to life, several factors contribute to this situation, all of which we will conquer throughout this book:

Lack of Clarity: As you progress in your career, you may find that your initial goals and aspirations no longer align with your current circumstances or interests. This lack of clarity about your direction can lead to feeling stuck or unsure about the next steps.

Plateaued Growth: Career growth may slow down or become stagnant after a certain point. Promotions and opportunities for advancement may be limited, or you may feel you are being stifled, leaving you feeling stuck in a particular role or level.

Burnout and Fatigue: Mid-career women often face increased responsibilities, higher workloads, and the challenge of balancing personal commitments. This can lead to burnout and exhaustion, making it challenging to find the motivation or energy to pursue new opportunities.

Fear of Change: Mid-career women may have established a certain level of stability, comfort, and financial security in their current roles. The fear of stepping out of that comfort zone and taking risks can prevent you from exploring new paths and getting unstuck. We will tackle this head-on in chapter nine.

Limited Networking and Connections: Mid-career women may have a narrow network compared to when they started their careers. Building new connections and accessing opportunities can be more challenging without a robust network. This is going to be a big opportunity for me as I consider my *Next.* As more of a natural introvert, I haven't fostered as many connections outside of my organization as I should have.

External Expectations: Mid-career women often face external pressures and expectations from society, family, or peers. These expectations can influence decisions and make pursuing alternative paths or taking risks harder.

Restlessness: This is where most of my mid-career stagnation occurred. Every time I found myself stuck, it was related to an insatiable need to spread my wings, exercise bigger talent muscles, and feed my thirst for learning. This should be distinct from boredom. In every role, I had more to do than the hours in the day provided. However, there is a difference between volume and value. We will cover this detail further in chapter six.

Assessing Fit

Be yourself; everyone else is already taken.

— **Oscar Wilde,** Irish poet and playwright

Whether you are feeling stuck, restless, bored, or unfulfilled at work, throughout the balance of this book, we will unpack ways to move forward with intentionality. Unfortunately, the reality is that working hard and keeping your head down is not always enough to guarantee career progression, especially for women, who may face systemic barriers and biases in the workplace. Take the time to reflect on your mission, vision, values, passions, and long-term goals. Assess your current situation and identify areas where you feel dissatisfied or unfulfilled from three reflective points of view: culture fit, criteria fit, and talent fit.

Culture Fit: In the late 1990s, I was providing training to a high-tech company. I arrived that Saturday in my skirt-suit, stockings, and closed-toe pumps, professional and ready to go. The participants showed up in pajama bottoms, shower shoes, and tank tops, though equally present and eager. The tech company's culture was to come as you are when you felt most creative and deliver innovation. Ours was "Come in early, stay late, and follow the conservative standard." While I missed the memo on how to fit in with my client, it was an early lesson on the variations of organizational values.

Every company has a distinct culture, from Jack Welch's cutthroat, high-accountability days at General Electric to the nutty, dedicated culture of Herb Kelleher's Southwest Airlines. Understanding the cultural norms that best fit you is essential to your job satisfaction and success.

Furthermore, organizational cultures can change or evolve over time, particularly with leadership transitions. What may feel like a good fit initially could leave you feeling disconnected at a later time.

 Energize Self-Agency:

How consistently aligned are your core values with your current organization?

Keep in mind that looking forward does not mean you must change companies. If you work in an environment that fully represents your values, mission, and vision, your *Next* may be internal. Alternatively, suppose the culture does not align with your expressed values, mission, and vision. In that case, you will want to keep that in mind when we move to architecting your journey in chapter four.

Criteria Fit: Criteria fit is based on two learned or teachable attributes: knowledge and skills. Knowledge is the information you have gathered through education, experience, and effort. It is the cognitive understanding of information. Skill is the ability to put knowledge into action or apply the information in a specific way.

About a decade ago, while working in higher education, I wanted to hire someone for my team who had not yet finished her degree but who had raised triplets largely on her own, since her husband traveled for work. Due to her lack of an undergraduate degree, I received strong pushback from my institution; however, I insisted. Subsequently, the woman I hired is now in upper leadership in the organization.

Welch's grape juice did a study looking at the task of raising children and found that raising a child takes ninety hours a week, roughly 2.5 jobs before the parent even clocks in for work. My sister is a mother of multiples, so I know how those organizational skills get honed out of necessity, akin to operational skills born of military training.

When we seek to staff our organizations with the talent and skills needed to navigate the future of work—filled with complexity, ambiguity, uncertainty, and rapid and continuous change—we should tap more female leadership.

Heather E. McGowan, Future of Work Strategist, Keynote Speaker and Author

A study published in the *Harvard Business Review* found that women are less likely to apply for jobs if they do not meet *all* of the listed qualifications, as opposed to men, who will apply even if they meet only a third of the stated requirements. Women—and companies—often limit potential with arbitrary expectations. How should you think differently about all of your transferable skills and knowledge?

 Energize Self-Agency:

What minimum skills and knowledge do you feel will be necessary for career advancement?

Talent Fit: Talent is the non-teachable, hardwired, spontaneous pattern of thoughts, feelings, and behaviors, not acquired through effort or education, that provides intrinsic satisfaction and can be cultivated to near-perfect performance. This innate ability is most easily witnessed in sports or the arts. We can hear raw talent in a singer, see raw talent in an athlete, and taste raw talent in the culinary masterpiece of a blooming chef.

While talent in the workplace is more difficult to see or hear, the potential exists in all of us. When exercised, it results in a feeling of fulfillment and validation. What makes your heart sing?

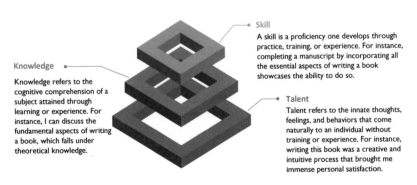

Skill

A skill is a proficiency one develops through practice, training, or experience. For instance, completing a manuscript by incorporating all the essential aspects of writing a book showcases the ability to do so.

Knowledge

Knowledge refers to the cognitive comprehension of a subject attained through learning or experience. For instance, I can discuss the fundamental aspects of writing a book, which falls under theoretical knowledge.

Talent

Talent refers to the innate thoughts, feelings, and behaviors that come naturally to an individual without training or experience. For instance, writing this book was a creative and intuitive process that brought me immense personal satisfaction.

Distinguish Natural Talents

Everybody is a genius. However, if you judge a fish by its ability to climb a tree, it will live its whole life believing that it is stupid.

— **Albert Einstein,** theoretical physicist

Imagine a world where every person was paid to perform in the area of their most extraordinary talent. Employees would be joyfully passionate, their customers would receive exceptional service, and the companies would reap the financial and reputational benefits. However, past studies by Gallup suggest that one in three employees feels miscast in their role. They are not serving in a position that fully leverages their natural talents, skills, and abilities.

Benefits of Exercising Natural Talent

There are numerous benefits and advantages when pursuing career growth in an area of natural talent. Here are some of them:

Greater potential for excellence: When you focus on developing your natural talents and skills, you can build upon a foundation that comes more naturally to you. This can lead to a higher level of proficiency in your chosen field. By leveraging your innate abilities, you increase your potential to excel and stand out among your peers.

Intrinsic motivation and fulfillment: Engaging in work that aligns with your natural talents often brings a sense of intrinsic motivation and fulfillment. When you're doing something you're naturally good at and enjoy, it's more likely to energize and inspire you. This can enhance your overall job satisfaction, boost your enthusiasm, and increase your sense of purpose in your career.

Faster skill development: Building on your natural talents allows for a smoother and quicker skill development process. You may find it easier to acquire new skills and knowledge in areas that resonate with your innate abilities. This can expedite your career growth, as you can progress more efficiently and confidently.

Enhanced creativity and innovation: When you work within your natural talents, you can tap into your creative potential more effectively. Your unique perspective and problem-solving skills can contribute to innovative solutions and fresh ideas. This can open doors to new opportunities, help you make meaningful contributions, and drive positive change in your career and industry.

Increased confidence and self-belief: Pursuing a career that aligns with your natural talents can boost your confidence and self-belief. Seeing your skills and abilities flourish in your chosen field can enhance your self-esteem and provide a keen sense of self-assurance. This can positively impact your well-being and empower you to take on new challenges and responsibilities.

Competitive advantage: By capitalizing on your natural talents, you can gain a competitive edge in your chosen field. Your unique strengths and abilities set you apart from others and make you an asset. You may find it easier to differentiate yourself, attract opportunities, and achieve success than those lacking natural inclinations do.

Grounded in your mission, vision, and values, your natural talent represents your true superpower. When cultivated, your gifts provide the foundation for your brand. Being distinctive requires clarity and confidence in the inherently talented and unique *you*. The only sustainable competitive advantage is aligning your talents in the right place at the right time!

Your Talent Spotlight

I had the opportunity to try something different that I thought I would like. Unfortunately, it wasn't what I thought. Almost immediately, I knew not to stick around, which is terrible on the résumé. But I knew that I couldn't stay in that position long-term. Based on my talents, I knew I needed something that would have a bit of a driver. That was going to be a challenge. I have a somewhat competitive spirit. I wanted something that allowed me not to feel like I knew everything; I needed to ask questions.

— **Beth Fredrich,** Director Marketing & Communications

In partnership with Future Workplace,® throughout 2022, Talent Plus® extensively studied the future of work. Leader insights regarding the talents that will be required for billions of current and future jobs were collected. Talent Plus® has featured this data at Future Workplace® summits and has been published in the *Harvard Business Review.*

Talent Plus® uncovered which talent themes will be most needed for the future workforce in canvasing and analyzing the job market and the future of work. With the influx of technological advancements like robotic process automation, machine learning, and artificial intelligence, the research predicts the employment market will shift to primarily knowledge workers. Talents like agility, learner, achiever, change agent, and authentic relationship builder will be essential for success in the workforce of tomorrow.

Employing more than fifty years of behavioral science, experience, and current research, Talent Plus® crafted a unique QR code provided at the end of this book, you can participate in the Talent Spotlight TOA® for our discounted price of $12 and reveal your natural gifts and talents.

Talent Card. | **Alexis Freeman**

The Talent Card captures your strongest talents and provides a pathway to help you understand your potential and assist in leveraging these strengths toward enhanced productivity and engagement. Your talents are listed in rank order.

Your Talent Creates Excellence

Developer — People Acumen

Coach, teacher, mentor - You instinctively nurture, coach, and mentor, unlocking potential in others. Your dedication elevates performance by empowering others to flourish and grow from consistent strengths investment.

How you express this talent
+ Elevate your success by empowering your team with engaging responsibilities and ownership that boost commitment and results
+ Your commitment to coaching and elevating others is a beacon of inspiration, deeply valued by those you guide towards success
+ Your success and fulfillment comes from nurturing others' talents around you, which allows your team to achieve extraordinary success

How to strengthen this talent
+ Continue to establish mutual trust with your team based on your actions and examples
+ Enhance your leadership by assembling a powerhouse team of eager-to-grow top performers committed to personal and professional development
+ Highlight the successes of your team and how honored you feel to coach and develop people

Talent Category

People Acumen
Reveals the extent, depth and impact of a person's interactions in both positive and negative settings.

Achiever — Drives & Values

Self-driven performer - Driven by a relentless motivation, you actively tackle challenges. Each obstacle is an opportunity for growth and excellence, pushing you to set and achieve new goals.

Mastery — Work Style

Adept, precise, and meticulous - Every task, even the most repetitive, is executed with finesse, ensuring accurate details and nearly flawless results. Your adept command over details guarantees exceedingly low margins for error, keying into important elements others likely overlook.

Purpose — Drives & Values

Loyal, committed and trustworthy - Guided by integrity, your actions reflect your commitment to principles and trustworthiness. Lead with purpose, inspire others, and excel in doing what's right.

Influential — Influence

Initiates direction and empowering - When the moment demands leadership, you confidently step up to guide the way. You make a remarkable difference by leveraging your deep conviction and shaping others' thinking as a role model.

Talent+.

The assessment will take approximately twenty-five minutes to complete and begin your strength development journey. Once you complete the Talent Spotlight TOA,® you will receive your custom Talent Card.® Click on one of the themes to expand the Talent Card,® revealing two sections. In this chapter, we will focus on the first section, "How You Express This Talent," and in chapter five we will address the second section, "How to Develop This Talent."

Undertake the challenge to make room for professional investment in you. Schedule uninterrupted time in the next two weeks to participate in the online assessment. If you do not choose to participate in the Talent Spotlight, you can refer to all of the themes in the appendix and identify the five that resonate most with you. While we can't guarantee the validity of your choices, it will give you a place to start.

 Energize Self-Agency:

Based on the talent spotlight, make note of your top five talent themes.

Talent Spotlight Themes

The Talent Spotlight includes five dimensions within which twelve themes are measured. As you reflect on section one and move through the remaining chapters, you may find that the more naturally your talent aligns with the subject, the more intuitive and comfortable the tips feel. For example, if you have a strong Purpose theme, chapter two likely resonated with you.

Conversely, in chapters where you find the recommendations are uncomfortable or counterintuitive, we may be pushing you in an area of lesser natural talent. Perhaps Caring is your number one talent theme, and you have softer Command. Asking you to put your needs first and establish healthy boundaries, as we did in chapter one, may have felt very challenging.

Pay attention to the topics that feel more natural and those that are pushing you out of your comfort zone. We will address the notion of Aces (strengths) and Spaces (gaps) later in this chapter. For now, just appreciate that some things will feel harder than others. We aren't going to recommend spending time developing a gap; however, we will encourage you to find ways to prop it up, allowing you more time to lean into the advice that plays to your strength. You may reference the talent spotlight theme and chapter crosswalk, which is near the end of the book and available in the *Now, Near, Next* Companion Guide.

Only your top five most intense themes will appear on your Talent Card.® This does not mean that the other themes are softer areas of talent; they are just not among your top five. Research suggests that 80 percent of how you show up can be identified in your top five leading themes. We will speak more to this in chapter four.

Alignment of Talent to Role

People who focus on using their strengths are **THREE TIMES** *likely to report having an excellent quality of life and* **SIX TIMES** *likely to be engaged in their jobs.*
— **Gallup,** *2020*

As you assess your current situation and consider your *Next*, it is as important to ensure an alignment with your top talents as well as the ability to mitigate that which doesn't come naturally or bring you intrinsic satisfaction.

Many years ago, I had the incredible blessing of working in an organization that successfully spun off its internal training and development department into a profitable third-party business. As one of the instructional designers and facilitators, I was often asked to attend sales calls to discuss the programs we offered. While I hated "sales," at least how I defined it then, this was more about sharing information and my expertise.

As the business grew, I was promoted to director of client development. My new role required calling on clients, discussing additional programs that may be of value, and performing against a sales quota, none of which appealed to me. Unfortunately, I was promoted into a position that no longer made my heart sing. Not long after, I left for a role more aligned with my gifts and aspirations. There are at least three primary reasons that people find themselves in positions that don't fully connect to their natural talents.

Misalignment: You can perform; however, the work does not bring you joy.

My son, Jacob, was an incredible baseball player when he was little. He always has had exceptional hand-eye coordination. When he was twelve, he no longer had the desire to play. While he had natural talents that aligned with performance on the field, he did not have the drive and competitive spirit for the game.

Today, he is a licensed drone operator, graphic designer, videographer, and video editor. His natural talents of physical dexterity are aligned with his creative gifts. Being able to do something with excellence and having a passion for the work is when your talents are aligned.

Another example of misalignment can occur when you have "graduated," and it is time to move up or on. Throughout mid-career, otherwise ambitious women may become so busy with life that the ideas of changing jobs or seeking a promotion feel overwhelming. Instead, they stay in a role that they can perform with their eyes closed. Every day is rinse and repeat. Instead of tapping their talent, they cap their talent. Eventually, this leads to boredom, or worse, malaise.

Have you ever been in a position where you could perform the task with ease, but it didn't make your heart sing?

Miscast: You are promoted into a position beyond your natural talent, sometimes called the Peter Principle.

Many years ago, before my understanding of talent science, I had an incredible executive assistant. She was driven and intelligent, and she had tremendous attention to detail. Wanting to reward her for her performance, I promoted her to a technical writer position.

She began to miss deadlines, underperform, and become disengaged, and I grew frustrated. I didn't understand that I had moved a top performer into a role that did not come naturally. Fortunately, there was an opportunity to recast her before she left voluntarily or involuntarily.

Have you ever been in a position that required talents that did not come naturally?

Misdirected: You have the motivation or interest (money, title, prestige, power) without considering or understanding the required natural talents.

When Jordyn was about eight years old, she professed from the back seat of the car that she knew what she would be when she grew up. She wanted to be one of those people who everyone told their problems to. When I inquired why, she shared that at school, all the kids told her their problems, and she knew exactly what to tell them to do! I explained that therapy and counseling are remarkable professions. However, they require much listening and asking questions to allow the client to reveal their best path forward. There was a long, pregnant pause from the back seat before she eventually exclaimed, "Well, what is a job where I can do all of the talking?"

When not aligned with natural talent, pursuing advancement

in a particular area of leadership, role, or industry for prestige, money, or title may prove difficult or unfulfilling.

Conclusion

Revealing your zeal requires a concerted effort to look up, a commitment to introspection, and the desire to move forward. By looking up and forward, you are identifying where you should focus your energy for the greatest return on your investment of time. Self-agency is realized when you choose the environment where you thrive, align your talents to your mission, vision, and values, and express a fully authentic self.

Remember that while natural talents provide a strong starting point, it's still essential to continuously develop and refine your skills through practice, learning, and experience. Combining your innate abilities with intentional growth can lead to remarkable achievements in your career.

With a clear sense of who you are and what you have to offer, it is time to actualize your growth by planning your *Now, Near, Next*, developing your strengths, and amplifying your aspirations.

Reflection: Reveal Your Zeal

My father taught me early in my career that when you are naturally passionate about the company you are working with or the product or service you represent, you are happier and ultimately more successful.

—Amy Zuckerman, Senior Vice President of People

After over thirty successful years as a human resources professional, Amy is an intuitive and authentic leader with extensive generalist experience in luxury and retail. She has scaled and built successful teams with a variety of acquisitions throughout her career. Currently, she leads a multibillion-dollar publicly held global retail organization. With a master's degree in organizational psychology, she balances the needs of the employees and business needs for maximum productivity and personal achievement. She recently parlayed her passion for yoga into Registered Yoga Teacher certification to assist employees on their mental health journeys. Amy currently lives in New Jersey with her husband and two Sheepadoodles. She and her husband enjoy time with their two grown sons, traveling and relaxing at their beach house.

After applying for my first job in a retail hardware store as a cashier at sixteen, I went home, and my dad, a psychologist, looked at me and said, "I'm so proud of you, but will you be happy working at a hardware store? Why don't you work with a product that you like?"

My father was brilliant. There was so much wisdom in his questions. You must work with products or services you are passionate about. It's a core theme in everything I've ever done. That was my first lesson. So where did I end up working instead? I worked for a luxury jewelry company and cherished every second.

It made perfect sense to me. I always loved fashion. I always loved high-end luxury products. My mother used to say she didn't know where it came from, because she liked discount shopping. I used to say, "Can we please go to Saks Fifth Avenue?" As a little girl, I would say, "I will work on Fifth Avenue one day." I don't know why, but I knew this felt right as I would stroll on Fifth Avenue during the school holidays.

From the first minute I interviewed with the HR professional at the jewelry store, I knew I wanted her job. I just knew. It was interesting because she interviewed me while setting up register training for new employees. She was also consoling two women who were arguing over a commission. I didn't even know what commission was at the time; I just knew she was trying to resolve a conflict.

I got the cashier job and immediately knew there was something about being able to help people in this type of environment that I loved. While working as a cashier, if it was slow, I found that I had a natural talent for selling beautiful products I was passionate about. And so at sixteen years old, I was selling thousands and thousands of dollars' worth of jewelry, earning big commissions for the actual salespeople! Now they were arguing over whose number I would use to ring the sale up!

I later followed in my parents' footsteps and earned a degree in psychology. I did think about being a clinical psychologist at one point. But again, my dad sat me down and said, "While you love to help people, you also like to understand business; why don't you think about where you can have the most significant impact on people and use all sides of your brain?" And that's what led to graduate school for a master's in organizational psychology.

My father taught me early in my career that when you are naturally passionate about the company you are working with or the product or service you represent, you are happier and ultimately more successful. His advice led me to a degree in organizational psychology and a career in human resources, where I could balance my love for helping people with my passion for consumer-facing businesses.

If I were to advise my younger self, I would share my father's incredible advice. Be true to yourself, stick with your passion, be loyal, work hard, keep learning, and share generously what you know. (And if you can make people laugh along the way, even better.) And don't ever let anyone ever underestimate you! Finally, although things may not always go your way, it's important to be resilient, pick yourself back up, and continue to move forward—after all, it's your journey!

Section One: Now—Energize Self-Agency

Take a moment to consider all the ways we have addressed energizing your self-agency in section one. Pause to revisit the personal reflections. Using the *Now, Near, Next* Companion Guide, or a journal, check to ensure you have documented all the quick action steps and created accountability for yourself. In addition, there is fundamental effort required to chart your *Now, Near, Next.* At a minimum, jot down first drafts or words and phrases that speak to you. As you continue through section two, you will be drawn back to your *Now, Near, Next Blueprint* on several occasions and can continue to develop your thoughts.

 Personal Reflection

 Take Immediate Action

 Chart in *Now, Near, Next Blueprint*

Chapter One:

 In what specific situation can you give yourself grace by

reframing your mental model from "I feel guilty about" to "I made this choice so that"?

💭 What one area of your life do you need to protect with a boundary of positive energy?

💭 How often do you reject help because of a false narrative?

🦶 When you inventory the significant responsibility of household chores, caregiving, and emotional support, what one thing could you delegate starting immediately?

💭 How can you minimize time spent with negative people who may influence your attitude, mood, and positivity?

🦶 What is one way that you will generate more positive energy in your life?

Chapter Two:

🦶 Identify your core values.

🦶 Author your concise and compelling mission statement.

🦶 Define your vision for the future.

Chapter Three:

💭 How consistently aligned are your core values with your current organization?

⛰ What minimum skills and knowledge do you feel will be necessary for career advancement?

⛰ Based on your talent spotlight assessment, make note of your top five talent themes.

SECTION TWO

Near—Ignite Intentionality

"Section Two: Near—Ignite Intentionality" moves to action. Chapters four through six reveal the importance of engaging the support of others, proactively investing in professional development, and ensuring your superpowers remain relevant. Your near may be over a six-month or a two-year time frame. There must be momentum forward and intentional iteration.

CHAPTER FOUR

Architect Your Journey

I have no small dreams!

— **Jordyn Schnieders,** my daughter

MY DAUGHTER, JORDYN, began performing in musical theater at an early age and aspired to be an actress. One day she shared with me that she had figured out what she wanted to be if her dreams of the big stage did not work out. Given her love of children, I thought she had a more practical idea, like a teacher. Instead, she professed that she would be a "female stand-up comedian!" Surprised, I laughed and suggested that her backup plan was more challenging than her primary dream. She replied, "Mom, I have no small dreams." From the mouths of babes!

At what point do we begin to minimize or dilute our ambitions— or worse, dampen those of others? As we have shared up to this point, our findings suggest that as life grows in complexity, we adjust our aspirations to the immediate future, at some points not beyond the week. Nearly every woman we interviewed stated that they were less intentional about their career planning and spent considerably less time investing in themselves and their growth than they would like.

Research conducted by Cornell University estimates that the average adult makes approximately 226.5 decisions a day about food alone. In addition, the data suggests we make 35,000 conscious decisions each day, from deciding what to wear to whether we should exercise.

Igniting intentionality in your professional development, which is guilt-free, empowering, and aligned with your talents and values, is a choice. Instead of defaulting to statements like "I don't have time" or "I don't have the energy to invest in one more thing," we can transform investing in ourselves into one of the many decisions we make each day to which we say yes.

Chapter four challenges you to proactively invest in your potential by developing a road map for your *Now, Near, Next,* creating an intentional strength development plan, and regaining that uninhibited agency to share your big dreams with the world.

Chart Your Now, Near, Next

Start by doing what's necessary; then do what's possible; and suddenly you are doing the impossible.

— Saint Francis of Assisi, Italian mystic and Catholic friar

As you begin the intentional effort to chart your *Now, Near, Next,* you must begin with the same grace we encouraged in section one. The most crucial goal throughout section two is to be intentional and make forward progress. You will determine the pace, the timeline, and the path based on what works best for you now.

As you begin to document your commitments in the *Now* and *Near,* do so with the following in mind:

Set goals: Develop specific, measurable, achievable, relevant, and time-bound (SMART) goals that align with your values and long-term vision.

Prioritize self-care: Prioritize your physical and mental health and find ways to manage stress and prevent burnout. Taking care of yourself will help you stay motivated and focused on achieving your long-term goals. We will emphasize this again in chapter nine.

Track your progress: Regularly review your progress toward your goals and adjust your plan as needed. Celebrate your successes along the way and use any setbacks as learning opportunities.

Determining What Is Next

The beliefs we perpetuate in corporate America suggest that success is determined by which rung you are on. We create a false narrative that the climb is narrow and steep, with little room to share. The reality is that we are far too versatile, exciting, and capable to allow these limitations. We open a world of possibilities by fully understanding our unique gifts and talents and intentionally planning for our *Next* with thoughtful discernment.

Early in my mid-career, I made a very intentional move from an international head of human resources to a lesser salary and narrower position. Having worked for privately held organizations for the first fifteen years, I felt that I needed to diversify my experience and move to a larger, public company. My children were at the ages of transitioning schools, and moving to a new area made sense. The transition was pivotal in my career trajectory.

Don't limit yourself to a vertical path. We so often fall into the trap of the proverbial career ladder. We adopt the idea that there is only one way up. We devalue the benefits of opportunities that widen our point of view if they are not within a traditional career progression. Dream with a horizontal and vertical mindset regardless of where and when your *Next* occurs.

The culmination of section one, "Energize Self-Agency," has prepared you to give voice and life to your *Next*. As you reflect on your mission, vision, and values, consider your natural talents and embolden your individualized brand. What is your *Next?* Your *Next* may be within or outside your current organization. Based on the assessment of fit in your current circumstances, your *Next* may be within a year or three years away.

When identifying your *Next* career move, several principal factors must be considered. Here are some key considerations:

- Reflect on your **talents, passions, and values.** Determine what kind of work fulfills you and aligns with your core values. Consider the activities or subjects that excite you and make you feel motivated.

- Reflect on your desired **work-life balance and lifestyle.** Consider factors such as work hours, travel requirements, and the level of flexibility needed. Determine how your career choice will impact your personal life and whether it aligns with your desired lifestyle.

- Ensure that your career move **aligns with your life goals** and aspirations. Consider how your career choice fits into the bigger picture of your personal life, relationships, and other life goals you may have.

- Assess your skills, strengths, and expertise. Identify your areas of proficiency and the skills you enjoy utilizing. Determine how to **leverage these skills** to enhance your performance and job satisfaction in your next career move.

- **Assess the potential for career growth** and development in your chosen field. Consider the opportunities for advancement, learning, and professional development. Determine whether the field you're interested in offers the potential for long-term growth and if there are opportunities to expand your skill set.

- **Evaluate the financial aspects** of your career move. Consider your desired career path's earning potential, compensation packages, and benefits. Assess whether the financial prospects are aligned with your goals and expectations.
- **Consider your risk tolerance** and willingness to step outside your comfort zone. Some career moves may involve taking calculated risks such as changing industries or starting a business. Evaluate the level of uncertainty you're willing to embrace and the potential rewards that come with it. We will address this in greater detail in chapter eight.

Let's explore an example in practice.

As I considered my *Next,* I knew I wanted and needed to remain in my corporate position for four to five years (financial). Knowing that I would never "retire" completely, I began exploring alternative ways to serve post-corporate life (interests). My passion for amplifying the gifts of women was something that inspired me (passion). Using my experiences from thirty years as an executive and my education in social psychology, I embarked on authoring a book in my *Now* and setting up the infrastructure to support a consulting practice in my *Near* (skills, talent). I could imagine a future owning my own speaking and consulting business, which would afford me the flexibility to carve out time for my friends, family, and grandchildren (values). Planning for my *Next,* I worked with my financial advisor to create a path that fit within my timeline, goals, aspirations, and financial tolerance (timeline and risk).

Remember that the decision-making process for your *Next* may take time. And depending on how far into the future your *Next* begins, your aspirations may be more or less clearly defined. Be open to exploring different options, seeking advice, and adjusting your course.

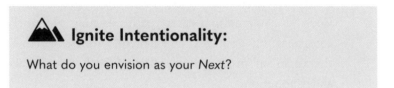

Ignite Intentionality:

What do you envision as your *Next*?

Begin with the End in Mind

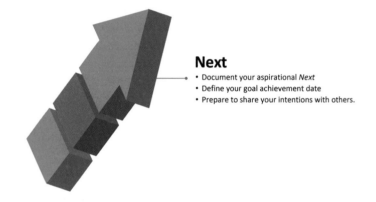

Next
- Document your aspirational *Next*
- Define your goal achievement date
- Prepare to share your intentions with others.

With your *Next* in mind, reflect on section one and your self-discovery thus far. The assessment of your current state will help to inform how much time you can dedicate to your personal growth *Now* and how much time you should allow before embarking on the *Near*.

Time: Chapter one, "Take Charge," means that you are dedicated to embracing grace over guilt, asking for and receiving help, and generating positive energy.

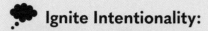 **Ignite Intentionality:**

How much time can you realistically, unapologetically commit to your growth in the *Now*?

Purpose: Chapter two moves you to proclaim your purpose. If you find yourself in a situation that is well aligned, you may have the luxury of time. Conversely, if you work in a company or role that conflicts with your sense of purpose, you may wish to accelerate your timeline.

Fit: Chapter three calls you to assess your culture fit, criteria fit, and talent fit. If you are learning, growing, and serving in a role that allows you to unleash your authentic talents, you may have more time to prepare for your *Next*. However, you may wish to hasten your plan if you are bored, restless, miscast, or otherwise stifling your talents and individuality.

How aligned is your current position with your natural talents? How would you rate the extent to which your job allows you to live into your full talent potential? You can assess how much you exercise your gifts in the workplace and where you desire to increase your focus by reflecting on the following questions:

Questions	Notes	Frequency	Score 1 (0–20%) 2 (20–40%) 3 (40–60%) 4 (60–80%) 5 (80–100%)
When reflecting on fulfilling days at work, what tasks or activities bring me joy and positive energy?		How much of my time is focused here?	
What types of work do others ask for my help with?		How often am I given this opportunity?	
For what types of efforts do I frequently receive compliments?		How frequently am I working in this space?	

As you consider your *Next*, you should be increasing the percentage of time that you are living into your natural talents.

 Ignite Intentionality:

To what degree does your current role allow you to consistently exercise your natural gifts and talents?

Reflecting on your current fit for the role, you can begin to determine a date by which you desire to move to your *Next*.

Remember, your *Next* could be with the same company or in a completely different industry. Your *Next* could begin in one year or five years. There is no standard or formula other than forward motion and momentum. Doing nothing, putting it off, and putting your head down are not options.

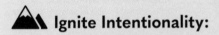 **Ignite Intentionality:**

When would you like the transition to your *Next* to occur?

There is something liberating about having a vision and a target date for your *Next*. If you are in a situation that is not filling your cup and know that you need to make a change, assessing your time, purpose, and talents enable you to put a plan in place. Even if you must stay the course for a period, channel your energy away from discontent and into positive momentum while continuing to perform in your role.

If you are in a place of contentment, having identified your *Next* keeps you from becoming complacent. Your window to a transition may be longer, but your intentional steps to move forward will keep you from waking up on the proverbial merry-go-round.

With a general timeline in mind, the remainder of section two provides essential tools and resources to help architect your journey. This section will encourage you to document your commitments on the *Now, Near, Next Blueprint*.

Moving from Now to Near

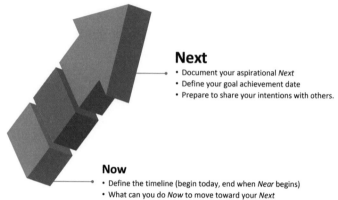

Next
- Document your aspirational *Next*
- Define your goal achievement date
- Prepare to share your intentions with others.

Now
- Define the timeline (begin today, end when *Near* begins)
- What can you do *Now* to move toward your *Next*
- Document your specific goals
- Prepare to share your intentions with others

With your *Next* target date in mind, you are ready to chart your path starting *Now*. As a rule, you will spend approximately two-thirds of the time before your *Next* focused on *Now* and the remaining one-third of your timeline in the *Near*.

Example

	1-Year Plan	3-Year Plan
NOW	9 months	2 years
NEAR	3 months	1 year

 Ignite Intentionality:

Based on your *Next* target date, take a moment to document the start date of your *Now* (today's date) and the start date of your *Near* (two-thirds of the time before your *Next*). Include this date on your *Now, Near, Next Blueprint*.

As always, availability is important when determining how much time you can invest *Now*. To get started, consider the things you can do *Now* that will begin to prepare you for your *Next* at a pace consistent with your timeline and current circumstances. Your *Now* will be focused on:

- Low-hanging fruit—tasks that are quick and easy to accomplish, e.g., updating your résumé, creating a LinkedIn profile, sharing your aspirations with those you trust
- Efforts that take longer to achieve but are foundational to your *Next*—courses, certifications, advanced degrees, authoring a book
- Building your support system—which we will cover further in chapter five

Example

	3-Year Plan	Action
NOW	Jan., Year One–Dec., Year Two	Establish an LLC Obtain Board Certified Coaching (BCC) credential Develop initial website Complete first book

Remember that the examples are from my *Now, Near, Next Blueprint* as I journey with you. Depending on where you are in mid-career, your goals may be focused on working toward a promotion, seeking a new role, or making a career change. Do not compare or attempt to replicate the illustrated actions. Rather, consider the type of actions they represent and how they grow in time commitment and pace as you get closer to your *Next*.

Ignite Intentionality:

Take a moment to document on your *Now, Near, Next Blueprint* some of the preliminary action items that you will focus on in the *Now*. You will continue to add to your *Now* action items as we move through chapters five through nine.

Preparing for Near to Next

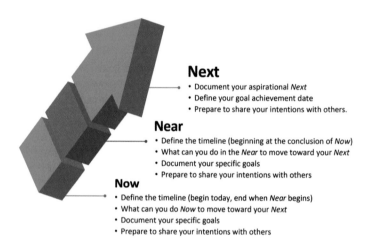

Next
• Document your aspirational *Next*
• Define your goal achievement date
• Prepare to share your intentions with others.

Near
• Define the timeline (beginning at the conclusion of *Now*)
• What can you do in the *Near* to move toward your *Next*
• Document your specific goals
• Prepare to share your intentions with others

Now
• Define the timeline (begin today, end when *Near* begins)
• What can you do *Now* to move toward your *Next*
• Document your specific goals
• Prepare to share your intentions with others

As you plan for your *Near*, remember that this is the ramp-up to your *Next*. You are accelerating at this point in your journey. As such, be mindful that your time commitment is greater and should be considered. Milestones are more significant, and outcomes are transitionary and potentially disruptive.

Your *Near* will be focused on the following:

• Bigger rocks—fewer efforts that take more time and energy, e.g., leading a large initiative, serving on a board of directors

- Efforts that take more intense focus, e.g., creating an online presence, publishing articles
- Building your network—more intentional focus on developing strategic relationships and serving on a volunteer committee, which we will cover in chapter five
- Broadening your perspective—seeking ways to contribute within and outside of your organization and industry, which is addressed in chapter six

Example

	3-Year Plan	Action
NOW	Jan., Year One–Dec., Year Two	Establish an LLC Obtain Board Certified Coaching (BCC) credential Obtain ICF credential Develop initial website Write first book Market book, light public speaking Engage in financial planning Engage supporters Serve on nonprofit board Identify public board seat opportunities Begin second book
NEAR	Jan.–Dec., Year Three	Develop a business and marketing plan Broaden network Increase public speaking Advance website design Strengthen financial plan Seek public board opportunity Develop podcast

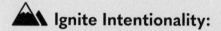

Ignite Intentionality:

Take a moment to document some of the preliminary action items you will focus on in the *Near* on your *Now, Near, Next Blueprint.*

You will continue to add to and refine your *Near* action items as we move through chapters five through nine. Remember, this is intended to be intentional and planful. However, if you have recently experienced a significant change, e.g., recent promotion or job loss, delaying or accelerating your *Next* may be necessary. The concepts still apply, but the timing will vary. And because life happens, we will unpack resilience and flexibility in chapter nine.

Create a Strengths-Development Plan

Don't try to teach a pig to sing. It's a waste of your time, and it annoys the pig.

— **Mark Twain,** American author and humorist

More than 60 percent of the women we surveyed and nearly 100 percent of the women we interviewed admitted to not spending enough time on strength development. "Strength development" refers to identifying and nurturing individual strengths and talents. In positive psychology, strengths are innate qualities that contribute to a person's positive functioning and well-being. Examples of strengths include creativity, perseverance, leadership, and problem-solving abilities. By recognizing and leveraging your strengths, you can enhance your performance, engagement, and satisfaction in various domains of life.

Strength development involves self-awareness, self-reflection, and deliberate practice to enhance and apply strengths in different contexts. Based on how much time you can unapologetically commit to your growth *Now* and the duration of time before your *Near*, identify the skills, experiences, and qualifications you need to acquire to reach your goal.

Shining Your Talent Spotlight

There is a difference between room for improvement and potential to improve. Working on areas of weakness yields minimal improvement after great effort. It undermines self-esteem. Working on areas of giftedness yields rapid growth, increased engagement, and enhanced self-esteem if the area of giftedness is something a person enjoys doing. It is a sign of intelligence and self-confidence to acknowledge what you are good and not good at, and what you like and do not like to do.

— Turnage and Sternberg, 2017

The law of the vital few, known more formally as the Pareto principle, helps people focus on the things that make the biggest difference. It is also known as the 80/20 rule. It states that roughly 80 percent of the effects come from 20 percent of the causes or inputs. The principle is named after Italian economist Vilfredo Pareto, who observed that approximately 80 percent of the wealth in Italy was owned by 20 percent of the population.

The Pareto principle has been widely applied to various fields and has shown that a small number of inputs or factors often contribute to a large portion of the outcomes or results. Here are a few examples to illustrate its application:

Business: In business, it is often found that approximately 80 percent of a company's profits come from 20 percent of its customers or products. By identifying and focusing on the most profitable customers or products, businesses can optimize their resources and increase overall efficiency.

Time management: The Pareto principle can be applied to time management as well. It suggests that roughly 80 percent of the results or value you achieve comes from 20 percent of your activities. By identifying and prioritizing the most important tasks or activities, you can maximize your productivity and minimize time wasted on less impactful activities.

You are now ready to create strength development goals by focusing on your **top five strengths**.

As you review your Talent Card,® identify the talent themes that positively impact your *Next*. Using the "strengthen this talent" section:

Developer
People Acumen ^

Coach, teacher, mentor - You instinctively nurture, coach, and mentor, unlocking potential in others. Your dedication elevates performance by empowering others to flourish and grow from consistent strengths investment.

How you express this talent

+ Elevate your success by empowering your team with engaging responsibilities and ownership that boost commitment and results
+ Your commitment to coaching and elevating others is a beacon of inspiration, deeply valued by those you guide towards success
+ Your success and fulfillment comes from nurturing others' talents around you, which allows your team to achieve extraordinary success

How to strengthen this talent

+ Continue to establish mutual trust with your team based on your actions and examples
+ Enhance your leadership by assembling a powerhouse team of eager-to-grow top performers committed to personal and professional development
+ Highlight the successes of your team and how honored you feel to coach and develop people

Talent Category

 People Acumen

Reveals the extent, depth and impact of a person's interactions in both positive and negative settings.

---

1. Ask yourself which of the three points most resonates with you as an area of opportunity.
2. Select one statement you want to focus on in your *Now.*
3. Select one to develop in your *Near.*

 Ignite Intentionality:

Take a moment to document a minimum of one strength-development goal to focus on in your *Now* and in your *Near.*

Addressing Aces and Spaces

It is important to remember that while strengths-based approaches have many benefits, it does not mean you should ignore your less natural talent altogether. A balanced approach includes recognizing and addressing gaps (spaces) while capitalizing on your strengths (aces) to help you create your *Near* and *Next.*

As you reflect on the talent themes that you identified as less intuitive, imagine ways to shore those up instead of wasting time and energy on marginal improvement. When you partner with others to round out your spaces, you amplify your collective natural talent and validate the other person.

- If you aren't naturally persuasive, share your idea with a trusted partner who is persuasive and influential. I tend to influence more through knowledge than persuasion, which isn't always successful by itself. To mitigate this, I frequently pull others of credibility into an idea or concept and build sponsorship. When we pitch the idea, I support the data and information, and my partner(s) bring the passion and real-world experience to the table.
- If you aren't particularly gifted with attention to detail, ask

someone to double-check your work. If you aren't a strong writer, hire an editor or ask someone to review and edit your most visible work.

- If you are more introverted, bring a colleague or friend to help work the room and keep the conversation going. Throughout my career, I have had to participate in a number of external events and fundraisers. I've had little trouble finding a friend or associate willing to join me. There is a little extra comfort in having someone share the spotlight.

If your position requires you to perform frequently and consistently in an area of soft talent, you may want to reconsider fit for the role. You deserve to live into your gifts and talents and enjoy the exponential success of unleashing your superpowers.

Authenticate Your Brand

Don't be afraid to be your authentic self at all times.

— **Ayesha Khanna,** PhD, Cofounder and CEO, Addo

In my mid-twenties, I had the incredible opportunity to work with a woman who embodied many qualities I aspired to develop. During my tenure, she was the only female executive on the senior leadership team of a commercial real estate company. It would be an understatement to say that it was a male-dominated industry at the peak of the good-ole-boy era. Yet without compromise, she rocked her diversity and her talent.

Put together from head to toe, she was as radiant and beautiful as she was intelligent and tenacious. Her ability to command and control a room while delicately navigating the sometimes-tender male egos was artful. She could be direct, demanding, and at times, fierce. She was a force to be reckoned with; men respected her, and women admired her.

Women like her have built successful personal brands by being authentic, consistent, and passionate about their work. Defining a professional brand can help women establish themselves as experts in their fields, increase their visibility, and stand out in a competitive job market.

Conversely, as I mentioned in chapter one, some behaviors can lead to unintentional brand development. One of the women we interviewed shared that she never said no to taking on additional work. Everyone knew they could come to her if they needed something, and she would get it done. At one point, she described how she was doing the work of three people, and a day didn't go by that she wasn't stressed, overwhelmed, and crying. She admits that she had zero boundaries.

As you consider defining your distinct brand, inventory any behaviors that may be in conflict with what you desire to project. Changing old behaviors will be as important as amplifying new ones.

 Ignite Intentionality:

What new behavior do you wish to amplify? What old behavior will you choose to diminish?

Defining Your Distinction

My intersection is applied AI. Once you understand yours, you should have only three hashtags. Keep it simple. Mine are #artificialintelligence, #Girlsintech, and #HumancentricAI. That's it. That's all I believe in, and having that kind of internal adherence helps me upscale because then I know what I'm looking for and where I need to continue to focus my development.

— **Ayesha Khanna,** PhD, Cofounder and CEO, Addo

The essential element of enriching your brand is to be not only different but distinctive. Differentiating oneself focuses on establishing a unique identity and expressing individuality, while being distinct focuses on having qualities or features that make a person stand out or be recognized in a particular context.

Here are some steps to help you define your professional brand:

Be Authentic: Your professional brand should genuinely reflect who you are. Do not try to be someone you are not, as this can come across as inauthentic and undermine your credibility. Choose a company culture and role that fits your authentic self.

There is an author and public speaker on LinkedIn that posts regularly. She often includes glamorous pictures of herself in business attire that I would describe as overtly sexy. On a recent post, she stated, "If you don't like what you see, if you find me off-putting, unfollow." She was making a bold decision to own her brand unapologetically. I had the choice to continue to follow or unfollow, as do organizations.

Again, know your audience and choose a company culture that is consistent with your professional brand.

Be Visible: Use social media and other online platforms to establish your professional brand and connect with others in your field. Keep your profiles updated and on brand, and use them to showcase your skills, accomplishments, and thought leadership. Using explicit hashtags brings you into the conversation and establishes you as part of a community.

If your company has a social media department, ask for ideas or support to get your message out on behalf of the organization.

I've had the benefit of a terrific communications leader who helps identify opportunities to post content that is consistent with my brand and voice.

Be Memorable: Share concise and compelling messages that communicate who you are, what you do, and why you are unique. As mentioned in chapter two, reveal your values, mission, and vision. These messages should be reflected in your résumé, cover letter, social media profiles, and other professional materials. See how to develop an elevator speech in the following section.

Be Consistent: Your brand is expressed through how you show up, verbally and nonverbally. The clothes you wear, the words you choose, and the images you post all communicate something about your brand. According to Albert Mehrabian, 55 percent of what people trust about what you say comes through nonverbal cues. When there is an inconsistency between what people see (body language, actions) or hear (tone) and what you say (words), they will believe the former.

Many years ago, I had a training manager that was frustrated with her lack of career progression over her long tenure. She had essentially grown up in the company. Over the years, she had developed a reputation of being a party girl during company events. She also dressed provocatively, at least for the standards of the company at that time. Even though she was an outstanding trainer and a subject-matter expert and was exceedingly smart, she was not taken seriously.

When she sought my counsel, we discussed this reality. This was not the professional brand she wanted or intended. She made some significant changes over the next year in the way she presented herself. Ultimately, she left the organization for a next-level role in which she leveraged her professional brand.

Following these steps, you can define your professional brand and position yourself for success. Additional ways to expand your community and showcase your brand are addressed in chapter seven. Remember that building a professional brand is an ongoing process that requires continuous learning, self-reflection, and adaptation to stay relevant and competitive.

Establishing Your Elevator Speech

An elevator speech, also known as an elevator pitch, is a concise and compelling summary of who you are, what you do, and what you can offer. It is called an elevator speech because it should be short enough to deliver during a brief elevator ride, typically lasting around thirty seconds to two minutes. The goal is to capture the listener's attention and make a memorable impression. It can be used in various professional and networking settings to introduce yourself effectively.

Hello, I'm Kimberly, a human potentiality expert. I specialize in helping people worldwide unlock their professional potential, leading to increased learning opportunities, promotions, and greater fulfillment. By identifying individuals' strengths and passions, I empower them to excel and find joy in their careers. This fosters personal growth and has benefits for companies such as increased engagement, retention, and performance. If you are curious about how to create a talent-based organization, let's connect and discover the potentiality within your organization.

An elevator speech typically includes the following elements:

Introduction: Start with a brief greeting and introduce yourself with your name and professional background.

Value proposition: Clearly articulate what you do, the problem you solve, or the value you bring to others. Highlight your unique skills, expertise, or qualifications.

Benefits: Explain how your work or expertise can benefit others or solve a challenge. Emphasize the value or results that you can deliver.

Differentiation: Stand out from the competition by highlighting what sets you apart or what makes your approach unique.

Call to action: Conclude with a call to action such as suggesting a meeting, asking for further discussion, or providing your contact information.

Practice and refine your elevator speech to flow naturally and adapt to different situations. It should be concise and engaging and leave a positive impression.

Hello, I'm Cynthia. As an experienced strategic executive and social psychologist, I have helped numerous companies and hundreds of executives realize the exponential benefits of placing the right talent in the right place at the right time. Success is measured in performance outcomes, employee and customer delight, and profit dominance. If you want to elevate your organizational or professional brand for increased impact, let's connect and explore how I can support bringing your vision to life.

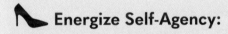 **Energize Self-Agency:**

Develop your elevator speech.

Amplify Your Aspirations

It takes a lot of courage to show your dreams to someone else.

—Erma Bombeck, American humorist and writer

Throughout my thirty-year career, I have had the great privilege of serving as an executive coach to current and former colleagues. More recently, I pursued a board-certified coach distinction in preparation for my *Next*. During a recent coaching session, an exceptionally talented leader stated her desire to succeed her boss, the head of the department, upon his retirement. As we discussed her *Next* and ways to develop her *Now* and *Near*, she expressed concern about her aspirations being interpreted as threatening to her boss and in competition with her peers. She struggled with amplifying her aspirations without being perceived as self-promoting and self-serving.

As we worked through her concerns, we first needed to dispel the narrative and the likelihood that her aspirational goals would fuel disruptive competition. Voicing her aspirations for her *Next* did not mean that others couldn't have a similar path. Instead, stating her desire was intended to seek support from her leader, who could provide meaningful feedback and opportunities for development. The intentional plan within her *Now, Near, Next* was personal and individualized to benefit her growth, not at the expense of others.

This interaction aligned with a study published in the journal *Psychology of Women Quarterly*, which found that women were less likely to express their career aspirations, mainly if they were in male-dominated fields. The study attributed this to the fact that women may face social backlash or negative stereotypes when they express their ambitions.

Take a Compliment

Oh, this old thing, I only wear it when I don't care how I look.

— **Violet (Gloria Grahame, actress),** *It's a Wonderful Life*

Early in mid-career, I was traveling for business and had the most memorable conversation with a fellow business traveler. I recall that the gentleman was much older than me at the time. He seemed polished, professional, and wise. He shared a piece of advice with me on that flight that I have never forgotten. "When someone gives you a compliment, simply say thank you."

He went on to say that he worked in a nonprofit on occasion with Marie Osmond, and he was always struck by her grace when receiving a compliment. She would say, "Thank you for saying that." Now, I can't validate that Marie Osmond in fact coined that phrase, but that advice never left me. Since that day, I have embraced and accepted positive feedback with that same genuine appreciation.

A study published in the *Journal of Personality and Social Psychology* found that women tend to downplay their successes and attribute their accomplishments to external factors. At the same time, men are more likely to take credit for their successes and attribute them to their abilities. Even among the many women we interviewed, success was often credited to luck or the influence of others.

However, it is essential for women to recognize the value of their talents and gifts and to take steps to promote themselves confidently. This can include practicing self-affirmations, seeking opportunities to showcase their skills, and connecting with supportive sponsors and mentors who can help them build confidence and visibility. By valuing your talents and presenting yourself confidently, you can amplify your potential and achieve your goals.

Be Humble *and* Ambitious

In many cultures, women are socialized to prioritize humility and selflessness, making it difficult to speak openly about their accomplishments or showcase their talents. One of my clients shared with me her desire to elevate herself to vice president. She had thoughtfully developed a job description for the next-level role and could clearly articulate the expanded responsibilities. She also understood that a next-level role would require growth in her department to be justified. She intended to share the proposed new role with her boss and state her interest in aspiring toward the opportunity should it become available.

I was impressed. She took the initiative to create the job description, was realistic about timing and the business need, and was planning to advocate for herself. However, she was nervous and uncomfortable with the *ask*. So we role-played the conversation with her boss, where she minimized her eligibility and successes.

There was a disconnect between her confidence in creating her aspirational job description and her passive approach to self-advocacy. She stated that culturally, she was raised with expectations of perfection and humility, never feeling good enough, smart enough, or pretty enough. She was concerned that others were qualified for an expanded role, and she would be seen as competitive, aggressive, or self-promoting in speaking up.

Advocating for yourself is not a competition with others. You enter the race when you share your aspirations, invite feedback and sponsorship, and are willing to put forth the effort to prepare yourself for the opportunity. However, you cannot expect people to read your mind. Sitting on the sidelines hoping for an invitation to participate will leave you behind.

Examples like this and numerous studies suggest that societal expectations and gender stereotypes can contribute to a lack of confidence and self-advocacy among women. Often justifying it as humility, women fail to speak up for themselves, articulate their goals, and seek opportunities that align with their aspirations. While humility is an honorable trait, it is essential to recognize that self-awareness and self-confidence are vital for achieving your goals and advancing your career. A clear understanding of your values and natural talents and a powerful sense of purpose allow you to share your interests and aspirations confidently. Leave nothing to chance.

Distinguish Self-Advocating from Self-Promoting

When Kimberly and I began writing this book, we wanted to gain interest from our respective networks. We began promoting various concepts through brief videos and blog posts on LinkedIn and Instagram. We were putting into the universe our plans and advocating for what we knew would be a benefit to mid-career women.

Even though the content was rich with insight, I recall feeling a little embarrassed when a colleague would bring up my social media presence or the impending book. While from many, the posts were met with gratitude and praise, there were those whose responses, directly and indirectly, suggested I was simply drawing attention to myself—self-promoting. In hindsight, I've resolved that this reaction has much more to do with the insecurity of the person casting judgement than with merit.

Self-promoting refers to bringing attention to oneself and one's accomplishments to gain individual recognition, visibility, or advancement ahead of others. It can sometimes be seen as self-centered or arrogant, and it can potentially damage one's reputation if done excessively or inappropriately.

Self-advocating is a form of self-assertion in which you advocate for what you are passionate about and for your needs, aspirations, interests, or rights. It involves speaking up for yourself, being visible, setting boundaries, and negotiating assertively but respectfully.

Highlighting your accomplishments or professing your aspirations without appearing boastful can be a delicate balancing act. Here are a few tips to help you showcase your achievements humbly and authentically:

Frame your advocacy in terms of service: Rather than focusing on yourself, focus on how your work can benefit others. Highlight how your skills and accomplishments can help the team or organization achieve its goals.

Focus on the results: Instead of discussing your accomplishments in terms of what you did, focus on your impact. Highlight the positive results that you achieved and the benefits that work.

Use objective metrics: Whenever possible, use objective metrics to quantify your accomplishments. This can include data on increased revenue, improved customer satisfaction ratings, or reduced expenses. This can help demonstrate the tangible value of your work.

Be concise: Avoid going into too much detail when discussing your accomplishments. Stick to the key highlights and be concise in your descriptions. This can help you avoid coming across as self-promotional.

Practice self-compassion: Recognize that self-advocacy can be uncomfortable and allow yourself to make mistakes or experience setbacks. Practice self-compassion and remind yourself that self-advocacy is a process, not a destination.

I had to learn to embrace self-advocacy and stop minimizing the incredible ambition of authoring a book. The fact is, I was not in competition with others or dimming someone else's light. I was shining a light for others, including, in theory, the company and people I was affiliated with. When I was questioned about our social media presence or the status of the book, I replaced my embarrassment and humility with confidence and gratitude.

"Thank you! We are so excited to be on a journey to help mid-career women look up and forward and put more intentionality into their professional advancement. My goal is that it will help not only the women in our organizations but also women around the world."

Overall, humility and self-advocacy are not mutually exclusive. By balancing the two, you can effectively advocate for yourself while remaining true to your values and personality. If you struggle with self-advocacy, seek a mentor or coach, the focus of the next chapter, to help you build the skills and confidence you need to advocate for yourself effectively. The key to highlighting your accomplishments without bragging is to be authentic and focused on your positive results.

Conclusion

Igniting intentionality begins with architecting your journey. The path forward should be at a pace and within a timeline that fits your circumstances, dreams, and aspirations. The most important consideration in architecting your journey is forward momentum.

With your *Next* in view, a purposeful strengths-development plan can be created. Taking a planful approach ensures more targeted growth and progress toward your goals. Instead of education and development for narrow subject-matter expertise, you are encouraged to think horizontally and expand your relevance.

With the clarity of your aspirations and path, you are encouraged to enlist fans, mentors, coaches, sponsors, and a network of people in your continued growth. Chapter five breaks down the differences between each of the types of supporters and reveals how engaging others in your plan is an essential element of igniting intentionality.

Reflection: Architect Your Journey

At the end of the day, your happiness is what matters, and it is what will lead you to success.

—Lisa Sterling, Chief People Officer, or a woman still trying to decide what she wants to be when she grows up

When I was a young girl and even into my early teenage years, my teachers would say I was too loud or that I was disrupting class. It was the same message from every teacher each time my mom attended a conference. I was the talkative one. I told stories, answered all the questions, and couldn't sit still. It drove my parents and teachers crazy until they learned to harness these strengths and leverage them in a positive way. That's when I began to flourish.

For most of my early career, I channeled my gregarious nature in ways that built relationships, expressed ideas, and exuded confidence. I was meticulous in taking on certain roles that many people questioned. Some said I needed to be more focused, to have a clearer path and stay the course. I am glad I didn't listen and went my own way.

I spent my entire early career navigating my way to a seat in the C-Suite. Once I had that coveted seat, I found myself unable to be loud, outspoken, boisterous. That outspoken, gregarious, disruptive young girl found herself a woman in unchartered waters.

I frequently wondered if I was having imposter syndrome or if I simply wasn't qualified to be at the table. I kept my ideas and perspectives to myself. I found my male counterparts speaking up, challenging others, all while I sat there, still and quiet. What had happened to me? Where was the confident, bold, disruptive person I had been just a few short months ago?

A woman with a voice is, by definition, a strong woman. But the search to find that voice can be remarkably difficult.

—**Melinda Gates,** American philanthropist

After the last executive meeting I sat in, I called my executive coach and said I was in need of a "911 call." I shared my story with her, and as soon as she started sharing her perspective, I knew exactly what I needed to do. I needed to give myself grace. I needed time to adjust to my new role, peers, and demands. My *Now* was different from my *before*, and I wasn't adjusting, pivoting, or expanding. I climbed this proverbial career ladder, and I just stood there.

So what did I do? I jumped off the ladder. I climbed into my role not as an executive but as a confident, capable, and outspoken woman leader. It doesn't matter what your title is, how big your W-2 is, or how many people you lead; what matters is the impact you make on people along the way.

As I think about my *Next*, I find myself excited, apprehensive, uncomfortable, and determined. It's completely acceptable if you don't have it all figured out. Be open to doing things you didn't plan. Don't let others keep you from expanding or pivoting. You do you. At the end of the day, your happiness is what matters, and doing what you love will lead you to success—no matter where that is on a ladder or lattice.

CHAPTER FIVE

Recruit Supporters

I don't lose sight of how it takes other people to help get you there.

— **Tiffany Owens,** Vice President, Human Resources

.

I LANDED MY FIRST BIG-GIRL CORPORATE JOB AT TWENTY-ONE, fresh out of college. The position was an assistant asset manager—a glorified title for an administrative assistant to a commercial property manager. That job, working for Nancy, set the course of my professional career.

Nancy was my first professional mentor. She was inclusive, smart, caring, fun, and respectful. I watched everything she did and listened to everything she said. She was a fierce negotiator, a natural conversationalist, and a mom. She set the example of how to be a respected woman in a male-dominated industry.

One afternoon, I was called into Nancy's office. Getting straight to the point, she informed me that the Dallas office was closing, and she and I would not have a job by the end of the following month. As my eyes filled with tears, Nancy leaned over her desk—all five feet, two inches of her—pointed her finger directly at me, and, with a bit of a smirk, exclaimed, "Don't you dare let them see you cry!" The "them" was the office full of male commercial real estate bankers, brokers, and dealmakers. The same men that had contests about which female assistants had the best legs, but that's a different book.

Whether you agree with Nancy's advice, it was a powerful coaching moment for me. I could stay in her office until I pulled myself together, but professionalism, confidence, mental toughness, and resiliency were expected when I walked out that door. There have been many moments throughout my career, under various circumstances, when that advice has served me well.

Nancy was also my first professional sponsor. I had fortuitously applied for a promotional position in San Diego without knowing the Dallas office was in jeopardy. As I pulled myself together, she challenged me to crush my interview in San Diego the following week and shared that she had already put in a good word for me with her California counterpart.

Nancy was a role model of strength and courage, and she challenged me to exhibit the same. She sponsored me at a time that was crucial in my career.

Chapter five encourages you to take a complete inventory of your community, bring more intentionality to your support system, and put your intentions into the universe so others can support your aspirations. Sharing your intentions with others is critical in making progress toward a goal. The importance of engaging sponsorship in your *Now, Near, Next* is about creating advocates.

Appoint Your Life's Board of Directors

A board of directors in business provides governance and strategic guidance, with a fiduciary responsibility to act in the company's best interest. A personal life's board of directors is a concept that applies the idea of a board of directors to an individual's personal life and career. It represents a group of trusted advisors, mentors, and supporters who provide guidance, feedback, and support in various aspects of life. While it may not have a corporate board's formal structure and legal responsibilities, it serves a similar purpose of offering strategic advice and accountability.

We can surround ourselves with individuals invested in our success without self-interest. These individuals come into our lives as coaches, teachers, clergy, family members, bosses, friends, coworkers, etc. They represent people you trust, respect, and admire who have had a prominent impact on your life.

Naming your life's board of directors can be a helpful metaphorical exercise to gain clarity, set goals, and make important decisions. This is not an actual board. Individuals do not need to be invited to join. These are individuals that *you* have identified as positively influential to your past, present, and future success.

Engage Your Life's Board of Directors

1. Write down the names of those people who have positively impacted your life and been formative in who you are today.
2. Reflect on a specific event or circumstance that best illustrates their positive influence. Write down one or two words that describe how each person touched your life.

3. To the extent you can, share with each person the prominent seat they have on your LBD and the specific reasons why.

4. As appropriate, ask for their commitment to continued support.

5. Depending on the relationship, you may establish a regular cadence for touching base to seek advice, share progress, and gain insights from your board members.

👠 Appoint your Life's Board of Directors (LBD).

Another way to engage your LBD is to bring them together for a weekend retreat or group dinner. A friend of Kimberly's made it her fiftieth birthday wish to meet in person with each living member of her LBD throughout the year. As she met with each person, she shared the special ways in which that individual had touched and formed her life.

Do not underestimate the value of your LBD in supporting your *Now, Near, Next*. In addition to cheering you on, your community can be some of the most robust connectors between you and opportunities. These people will shamelessly brag about you to others, promote your vision, and sell you better than you can market yourself. Sharing your *Now, Near, Next* with close friends and family will further open your world to possibilities.

 Ignite Intentionality:

Commit to contacting at least one member of your LBD to share your *Now, Near, Next*.

Share Your Gratitude

Many years ago, I sent a letter to my high school language arts teacher, Mrs. Frances Engelbrecht, and the superintendent of schools, Mr. Jack Brumley. Both educators had a significant impact on my life. Mr. Brumley took me more seriously than I took myself. Mrs. Engelbrecht held me to academic and performance standards that sometimes felt unachievable. They both saw potential in me that I did not fully see in myself.

In the letters, I shared the concept of the LBD and how they held prominent seats on my life's board. I provided examples of how they made an impact on my life and influenced who I am today. Those two letters reunited us and led to a few additional exchanges.

What an incredible gift to have had the opportunity to share my gratitude with each of them. Mr. Brumley passed away in 2019. Mrs. Engelbrecht is still with us at the time of this writing. I pray that she will have the opportunity to read my first book. My biggest literary accomplishment with her thus far was the B+ I received on my George Bernard Shaw paper. I'd like to think my *Next* would make her proud.

Engage Sponsors, Coaches, and Mentors

Don't let all of your heroes be internal. It is the network externally that opens opportunities.

— **Ana Brant,** Vice President, Customer Experience

While the words are often used interchangeably, there is a distinction between sponsors, coaches, and mentors. Sponsors are those individuals who organically advocate for you. Coaches are trained in the art of questioning and listening. Mentors often blend the two and serve as role models, feedback loops, and advisors.

So while you may encounter someone like Nancy in your life, who wears more than one hat, it is essential that you are intentional about recruiting and naming a variety of individuals who provide you with growth, development, guidance, and advocacy, both inside and outside of your organization.

Recruit Sponsors

Sponsors are individuals who have been exposed to your gifts and talents, recognize your potential, and know your goals. You are on their minds in meetings, social settings, or professional environments where opportunities are discussed or alliances are revealed. They nominate you for projects, committees, or promotions that align with your ambition or introduce you to people who could influence your success.

Sponsors can be instrumental in advocating for your career advancement. Additionally, they can help you gain visibility, navigate organizational politics, and access influential networks that may otherwise be challenging to tap into.

External sponsors are equally important. In the event you desire to change jobs, start a business of your own, or need to find a job, sponsors who are outside of your organization can play a huge part in setting you up for success. These individuals are not bound by the same company loyalties; they are invested in you.

How to Engage Sponsors

Several years ago, a female leader I had been exposed to and impressed by in various meetings invited me to coffee. She expressed her desire to engage more formally with female leaders from whom she could learn and develop. That coffee led to an ongoing relationship and an opportunity for me to understand her aspirations. Since then, on several occasions, I have advocated for her as a potential candidate for a new role or a project assignment. That coffee chat gained her a sponsor.

I, too, have sought sponsors, both inside and outside of my employers. Barbara Archer, a partner with Hightower Wealth Advisors, and I met through her service on a board that I was affiliated with. Barbara is a consummate entrepreneur who generously gives her time, talent, and treasure. She graciously agreed to meet with me and was eager to learn more about this book and our focus on elevating professional women.

In a matter of two hours, she had numerous ideas on speaking opportunities and making connections with other like-minded business leaders and offered great advice on starting a successful podcast—she has firsthand experience as the host of *Keeping the Well in Well-thy*, a passion project she started with her company. That one phone call and lunch resulted in a deepened friendship, tremendous learning, several connections, and a trusted sponsor.

Engaging professional sponsors to support your career aspirations involves building relationships with influential individuals who can advocate for you and provide guidance. Here are some steps to help you in this process:

- Look for professionals who have succeeded and possess the knowledge and connections you seek. These individuals should have exposure to your work and the influence to support your career growth.

- Ask for sponsorship by clearly articulating your career aspirations and the ways in which a sponsor could support you. Be specific about the support you seek, whether it's introductions to influential individuals, recommendations, or advice on specific career challenges.

- Regularly engage with potential sponsors through emails, social media, or industry events. Share relevant insights, articles, or industry news to stay on their radar and demonstrate your commitment to the field.

- Show professionalism, reliability, and gratitude throughout your interactions. Sponsors are more likely to continue supporting appreciative individuals who demonstrate their commitment to growth.

- Pay it forward: Once you have established professional sponsors, seek opportunities to help others in their career journeys. Act as a mentor or advocate for someone else and demonstrate your commitment to fostering a supportive professional community.

Remember, building sponsor relationships takes time and effort. It requires authenticity, dedication, and a genuine interest in learning from and supporting others.

Ignite Intentionality:

Who are the people in your organization, industry, or community who could positively influence your *Next*?

Bear in mind that sponsorship can be reciprocal. We are not suggesting inauthentic relationships purely for personal gain. These are relationships developed on mutual respect and the desire to lift another person.

Enlist Coaches

As noted earlier, one of the commitments I made when architecting my journey was obtaining a coaching certification. As an executive and human resources practitioner for thirty years, executive coaching was a natural fit for my talents, interests, and *Next.*

Through the process, I learned two significant lessons. First, coaching is not advice-giving or direction-setting. Coaching, unlike mentoring, relies completely on appreciative inquiry and active listening. The coach's job is to ask pertinent and provocative questions that lead to self-discovery and professional growth. Coaches provide a supportive and structured environment for you to set goals, develop action plans, and work toward your aspirations. The coach's core function is to unleash the human potential of their client.

Second, everyone needs a coach, even a coach. As part of my certification, I have spent countless hours barter-coaching. Essentially, coaches coaching coaches. Not only has this process expanded my network with incredibly talented, insightful women, but it has also richly impacted my growth and development.

Coaching allows you to work through complex decisions or interpersonal challenges or discern where to focus your *Next.* As you journey through your *Now, Near, Next,* consider engaging an executive coach, particularly when you need clarity. Many organizations will pay for executive coaching and appreciate your openness to ongoing development. Alternatively, several professional industry associations offer coaching programs.

Identify Mentors

We established a women's mentoring program within my organization a few years ago. On more than one occasion, a male executive would inquisitively ask about the purpose of a mentoring program dedicated to women. The answer is quite simple: women and minorities seek the advice and counsel of those with a shared life experience. There remains a lack of supply and increased demand.

In most companies, men can throw a rock and they are bound to hit a successful executive male leader, or they report to one. Women must look much harder to find a senior female leader to mentor them. And if you are looking for a minority leader, the pool is limited further.

While having at least one mentor with a shared life experience can be uniquely beneficial, the essential factor is that you have a variety of positive role models from whom to learn. The goal is to have several people in your life that provide support, guidance, and opportunities for personal and professional growth. Again, having mentors both within and outside of your organization is key. Should you have a conflict with your current employer or wish to make a job change, external mentors can be better positioned to support you.

Here are some key reasons why women should consider engaging with mentors:

Skill development: Mentors can offer expertise and insights that help women develop new skills or enhance existing ones. They can provide guidance on specific areas of expertise, offer constructive feedback, and share their own experiences to help you build competence and confidence.

Knowledge transfer: Engaging with mentors allows women to tap into the knowledge and experience of seasoned professionals. Mentors can guide career choices, share industry insights, and help you navigate professional challenges.

Networking opportunities: Mentors often have extensive networks, which can be valuable for women seeking new connections, career opportunities, or access to resources. Engaging with these individuals can expand your professional network, connect with like-minded individuals, and open doors to new possibilities. More on this later.

Support and encouragement: Mentors provide a supportive environment where you can seek advice, discuss challenges, and receive encouragement. They can be trusted confidants, offering emotional support, motivation, and a fresh perspective during challenging times or important decision-making processes.

Confidence building: Engaging with mentors can significantly contribute to women's self-confidence. Through their guidance, you can better understand your strengths, identify areas for improvement, and develop a positive mindset. This increased confidence can empower you to take on new challenges, seize opportunities, and achieve your goals.

Overcoming barriers: Women often face real or perceived barriers and biases in the workplace. Mentors can help you identify and navigate these challenges, providing strategies and support to overcome obstacles. As recently as this year, a young woman consulted me about sharing with her boss that she was pregnant. She feared that among her all-male team, she would be limited in her career advancement. We worked through the announcement, putting positive energy toward her *Now, Near, Next* and sharing her plan.

It's important to actively seek out sponsors, coaches, and mentors who align with your goals, values, and aspirations. By intentionally engaging with these individuals, you can receive the support, guidance, and opportunities necessary to thrive personally and professionally. However, you must be willing to listen, be open to feedback, and follow through. As an executive coach, I expect my clients to come prepared with a focused topic and clear expectations of what they wish to gain from each session. If they aren't "coachable" and willing to do the work, it is a waste of time for both of us.

 Ignite Intentionality:

Identify one supporter (sponsor, coach, mentor) with whom you will share your aspirations.

Expand Your Network

Maintain professional connections from college and wherever you did your professional degrees, because they matter. They can matter in different ways later, in ways you never anticipated.

—**Aisha Smith,** JD, Council

As I reflect on the incredible number of women that Kimberly and I have asked to invest in this project, I'm overwhelmed with gratitude. Over three hundred members of a women's affinity group and thirty women representing numerous different industries, four countries, five races or ethnicities, and over nine hundred years of professional experience contributed. While that is impressive, what brings Kimberly and me the most joy is that these extraordinary women are part of our network. These relationships developed as coworkers, clients, friends, professional associates, and business acquaintances and have been nurtured over one to twenty-nine years.

These women share an incredible willingness to shine their light for other women and a bond that has been fostered and maintained through a mutual passion. The fact that so many women gave so selflessly of their time, talent, and wisdom is a testimony to the power of networking, relationship-building, and investing in long-term connections.

Yet if you were to ask me how I feel about networking in the traditional sense, it isn't my favorite thing. I have been described as a competent extrovert. On my own, I don't particularly enjoy going to events where I don't know anyone and working a room. On the other hand, Kimberly is masterful at connecting and drawing energy from a room full of potential collaborators.

There are many ways to build and extend your professional network, whether you are introverted or extroverted. Find an approach that works for you and then dedicate unapologetic, guilt-free time to that investment. Broadening your network is essential for personal and professional growth, but it takes intentionality to expand your connections. Here are some strategies to help you broaden your network:

Attend industry events and conferences: Participate in conferences, seminars, workshops, and networking events related to your field of interest. These events provide opportunities to meet professionals from diverse backgrounds, exchange ideas, and build connections. If you are an introvert, go with a colleague or business associate. Or start with virtual events that allow you to build relationships.

Join professional organizations and associations: Become a member of a board which aligns with your industry or interests. Engage actively in their events, committees, and forums to connect with like-minded individuals and industry leaders. Volunteering to serve on a committee is a terrific way to build a few deeper relationships, making the larger events less overwhelming.

Utilize social media and online platforms: Leverage social media platforms like LinkedIn to connect with professionals in your field. Join industry-specific groups and participate in discussions. Share insights, ask questions, and engage with others to expand your digital network.

Attend workshops and training sessions: Participate in workshops, training programs, and skill-building sessions. These gatherings often attract individuals from various backgrounds, allowing you to interact and network with professionals with complementary skills or interests. Exchange contact information with those you wish to develop a connection. Some of my most recent professional relationships were developed from the coaching certification.

Seek out cross-industry connections: Don't limit your networking efforts solely to your industry. Look for opportunities to connect with professionals from other fields or sectors. Cross-industry connections can provide fresh perspectives, new insights, and potential collaboration opportunities.

Leverage existing connections: Reach out to your current network, including colleagues, friends, family, and alumni associations. Tell them about your professional goals and interests and ask if they can introduce you to individuals in their network who might be beneficial connections.

Be proactive and follow up: Proactively initiate conversations and follow up with individuals you meet. Maintain regular communication, help when appropriate, and seek opportunities to collaborate or share insights. Networking is an ongoing process that requires consistent effort and nurturing.

Ignite Intentionality:

Choose one way you will expand your network in your *Now* and one way you will expand your network in your *Near*.

Remember, building a network takes time and effort. Be genuine, supportive, and open to helping others as you seek to expand your connections. Focus on building relationships rather than simply collecting contacts, and always be willing to offer value and support to your network.

Conclusion

It can be overwhelming to look up, take inventory, and plan for what is *Next*, particularly if you have been looking down for a while. Remember, it takes a village and continued forward progress. You are surrounded by individuals who have loved, supported, challenged, and pushed you throughout your life. Appoint those individuals to your life's board of directors and onboard them.

Being intentional about others who journey with you is equally essential. Identifying sponsors who will advocate for you when you aren't in the room could catalyze your *Next*. Engaging a coach to help you gain clarity as you discern your *Next* can make the process more energizing and less daunting. And surrounding yourself with mentors who are invested in your success provides you a safe space to learn and grow.

As you build your network, you will be reminded how small the world truly is. You may find new sponsors, coaches, and mentors from your network. You may even meet someone who is eventually added to your Life's Board of Directors. Most importantly, you can create reciprocal relationships that positively impact your *Now, Near, Next.*

With clarity about your natural talents, a plan for development, and a community of internal and external support, chapter six encourages you to broaden your perspective through stretch assignments, collaboration, and service. It is time to put your words into action.

Reflection: Recruit Supporters

I strive to maintain a balanced approach to giving and receiving, recognizing the immense value in life's intricate tapestry.

— **Amy Towner,** Cofounder and CEO of Health Care Foundation for Ventura County

Amy Towner is the cofounder and chief executive officer of Health Care Foundation for Ventura County (HCFVC). She focuses on securing strategic public/private engagement to enhance and augment the Ventura County Health Care Agency (HCA)'s public safety-net system (Ventura County, California).

Amy has been a successful serial entrepreneur and industry agnostic. As a Larraine Segil Scholar and member of the Exceptional Women Alliance (EWA), she has been described as a woman who has walked the road less traveled. She has also been recognized by Pacific Coast Business Times *as a "Leader in Healthcare" awardee.*

In 2018, Amy earned her MBA from Pepperdine University's Graziadio Business School for Presidents and Key Executives. In 2019, she attended UCLA's Anderson School of Business Corporate Governance Program and earned Pepperdine University's Healthcare Leadership Certificate.

Amy's passion is mentoring women at Pepperdine and within the EWA worldwide network, cooking, traveling, and entertaining. She has three grown kids and prioritizes family, faith, and impact.

As it did for my grandfather, entrepreneurship runs in my blood. By age twenty-three, I owned and operated my first business. Along the way, I was fortunate to have a female mentor who guided and inspired me, instilling a powerful desire to pay it forward to other women. And pay it forward I did. As I continued to navigate the business world, I also dedicated considerable time managing the back office of my husband's financial business, which grew to an impressive $200 million in assets under management. All the while, I managed to raise our children and actively engage in my community through volunteering.

Whether volunteering in my kids' classrooms, assuming the role of PTA president, serving as the Cotillion Grade Chair, or becoming a member of the National Charity League, I didn't fully realize the network of individuals I was cultivating within my community. Through my acts of service, I unknowingly built rapport with the people around me. These relationships would play a crucial role in my future career opportunities and come to my rescue in times of disaster.

In 2017, my life took an unexpected turn. At forty-eight years old, my twenty-five-year marriage ended, and my three children were off to college. Meanwhile, I was deeply involved in cofounding and running a startup nonprofit organization. Everything I knew and relied on suddenly seemed to shatter, leaving me especially fearful about my financial security.

Instinctively, I felt compelled to pursue further education, so I applied and was accepted into Pepperdine University's Master of Business Administration program. Juggling this commitment with full-time work was difficult. My upbringing in a challenging divorced family taught me the importance of self-reliance. Building a diverse network of people with various ages, gifts, talents, and superpowers from all avenues of life was critical for survival, and education would help me continue to broaden the breadth of my knowledge and network.

I had no idea what awaited me as I forged ahead. On December 4, 2017, a year after my divorce, the devastating California wildfire "Thomas" roared toward the Pacific Ocean. I was out of the country on a business trip, unaware of the impending disaster. Only when my children called me from college, urging me to turn on the news, did I see the heart-wrenching images of my home engulfed in flames.

Staring at my computer screen in disbelief, I couldn't help but ask myself, "What am I going to do? Is this really happening?" Shock set in, and I could feel my head shaking as a visceral response to the harsh reality. Memories flashed through my mind—baby pictures of my children, precious family jewelry, and my grandmother's pressed glass sugar bowl—all lost in the blaze.

A difficult childhood familiarized me with trauma and gave me a survivor instinct. With a rapid shift in mindset from mere survival to thriving, I turned to my network for support. I caught the next flight back home and sent out a plea to any women willing to lend me size nine pumps, sheath dresses, and a crossbody purse so I could rebuild a professional wardrobe. I contacted friends for replacement hair products and makeup. My mentor rallied the sisters in the Exceptional Women Alliance to help assemble suitable business attire. I sought refuge at a friend's home, asking another to assist with the logistics. With all of this in motion, I resumed my work responsibilities.

Throughout this challenging period, I also contacted others affected by the wildfire. Over one thousand families in our community had lost their homes, and few had the fortune of an engaged and supportive network like mine. Grateful for the duplicate gifts I had received, I endeavored to share them with those in need. Giving has always been a fundamental part of my life—supporting my family, friends, and community. It was my turn to humble myself and accept help graciously so I could rebuild and eventually give back again.

My cousin reminded me that I had dedicated my life to helping others, and now, allowing others to assist me was essential. She encouraged me to embrace this moment of need, understanding that it would forge deep and meaningful bonds with the people in my life. She explained that the human spirit thrives on both giving and receiving. This experience would create lasting connections.

My cousin's words rang true.

In my mind, I visualized a phoenix rising from the ashes after the Thomas fire. Just as disruption presents opportunities in business, I realized I could apply the same principle to my own life. Out of the wreckage of my possessions, I discovered the opportunity to rebuild myself, a newfound gratitude for my family's health, and a renewed understanding of the natural balance between giving and receiving.

Through heartache, tragedy, and starting over more than once, I recognized the power of embracing diverse individuals who became an incredible community on life's journey. My sponsors, mentors, coaches, network, and community were a stabilizing force at every turn.

Today, the nonprofit organization I cofounded is strong and scaling. I purchased a new home from a friend's mother. I continue to be mentored while mentoring others, paying forward the support and guidance I received. I strive to maintain a balanced approach to giving and receiving, recognizing the immense value in life's intricate tapestry.

The truth is, life is messy. Unexpected life events will happen. It is in both times of celebration and times of need that your supporters will be a tremendous source of strength. Never underestimate the power of your community. Build, nourish, and be a reciprocal contributor to maintaining those relationships.

CHAPTER SIX

Broaden Your Perspective

When we live in fear of "Am I worthy of this next thing," "Am I worthy of this place I may go or what I might do," it can be one of the most damaging, limiting beliefs that we have. The fear of being capable of more or different can keep you from leaning into what you know might be the right next thing.

— **Kara Bunde-Dunn,** CEO, Karmic Leader

SEVERAL YEARS AGO, I had the opportunity to serve in an interim role as the regional human resources leader in one of the company's largest communities. This position reported to me, but I had never directly held the role. That next nine months forever changed my worldview of health care and operational human resources.

For the first time, I was experiencing a day in the life of an operational leader. The never-ending requests from the corporate office, the expectations of meetings, and what often felt like the disconnect between those at the bedside and those in the glass building were palpable. It was an experience that broadened and reshaped my perspective.

With a broader perspective, you are better equipped to consider multiple angles and approaches to a problem or situation. It helps you develop critical thinking skills by challenging assumptions and biases, encouraging you to explore alternative solutions and consider diverse perspectives.

Chapter six pushes you to broaden your perspective through various internal and external options that require self-advocating, raising your hand, and putting yourself in situations that build character and expand capabilities. Consider where and when these opportunities for growth fit into your *Now, Near, Next* plan. You don't have to do them all, but commit to doing something.

Stretch Your Reach Internally

If I didn't like the projects that I was working on or didn't like even the position I was in, I'd constantly ask for different things to do or try and take on different things and offload things that didn't make sense. And I'd always suggest alternatives to my boss and not just complain but strategize. How can we partner to make this a better experience for you and me?

— **Amanda Fedje,** business owner

So many women we spoke to shared stories of asking for more. One of our contributors shared that she asked to expand her role nine months into her new job. She was told no the first time. Eight months later, she asked again and was given additional responsibilities.

There are several compelling reasons why women should put themselves in situations that build character. By intentionally placing yourself in situations that expand your capabilities, you can challenge and overcome limiting beliefs, increase self-confidence and self-belief, and achieve greater empowerment.

Benefits of Raising Your Hand

By intentionally seeking opportunities that build character and expand capabilities, you can unlock your full potential, enhance your professional prospects, and cultivate a continuous growth-and-learning mindset. It enables you to overcome challenges, seize opportunities, and make meaningful contributions in your personal and professional lives. Here are a few examples:

Personal growth and development: Engaging in challenging situations helps women develop resilience, self-confidence, and a sense of personal accomplishment. By pushing beyond your comfort zone and taking on new challenges, you can develop new skills, broaden your perspectives, and discover hidden strengths, leading to personal growth and self-improvement.

On numerous occasions, I have rotated leaders from one assignment or role to another. The opportunity for these women to use their transferable skills and talents to experience a different environment has enriched their potential. It is important, however, that you are not waiting for someone else to make that decision. Keeping your eyes and ears open for rotational opportunities is key.

Professional advancement: Putting oneself in situations that expand capabilities can contribute to professional advancement. You can acquire new skills, knowledge, and experiences highly valued in the workplace by seeking opportunities to learn and grow. This can lead to increased job opportunities, career progression, and the ability to take on more challenging and rewarding roles.

Years ago, I had the opportunity to assume leadership responsibilities for two departments outside of human resources.

While I do not have a formal background in philanthropy or government relations, my business acumen and leadership talents were successfully transferable. The expansion of responsibilities broadened my marketable competencies beyond human resources and forged my path as a chief administrative officer.

Building a strong personal brand: Actively seeking situations that build character and expand capabilities allows women to shape and enhance their brand. By demonstrating a willingness to take on challenges, pursue growth opportunities, and continuously learn, you can establish yourself as a capable, driven, and adaptable professional. This can positively influence how you are perceived by colleagues, managers, and potential employers.

The more you raise your hand and seek opportunities to contribute, the more you will be considered. If a position opens in your area, offer to cover it in the interim. If there is a project that doesn't have a natural owner, volunteer to lead. In most organizations, you must demonstrate that you can do the work before you are actually promoted into the role. Find those opportunities.

Expanded opportunities and versatility: Women continually seeking to expand their capabilities are more likely to be considered for a wider range of opportunities. Acquiring diverse skills and experiences makes you a versatile professional who can adapt to changing circumstances, take on new responsibilities, and contribute to various roles or industries. This increases your options for career advancement and opens doors to new possibilities.

In discussing succession planning with one of my leaders, we explored the potential for her to grow into a new area of human resources. At our next meeting, she shared that she had begun a certification program in the area of specialty. Her proactive approach to expanding her skills and knowledge accelerated her potential for job expansion and increased her versatility.

Thriving in a fast-changing world: In today's rapidly evolving world, the ability to adapt, learn, and grow is essential. Putting yourself in situations that build character and expand capabilities equips you with the resilience, agility, and skills needed to navigate a dynamic and competitive landscape. It positions you to thrive in the face of change and uncertainty. We will explore resilience further in chapter nine.

Evaluating Volume versus Value

My boss said, "You are a natural people manager." I said "yes" but explained that I didn't want to take on the management of the distribution center, which was part of the operations team. That was just giving me more volume, not necessarily intellectual stimulation or a growth opportunity.

— **Amy Zuckerman,** Senior Vice President of People

When considering taking on additional responsibility at work, it's important to evaluate whether it will contribute to your professional growth and add value to your *Next*. At times, you may desire to expand your scope because you feel it elevates the status or importance of your role. Yet if not aligned, you can add volume to your plate without adding value to yourself or the organization. Instead of gaining intrinsic satisfaction, you have given up valuable time.

I have been guilty of this throughout my career. Because I love leadership, team-building, and problem-solving, I would raise my hand whenever a department was without a leader. What I learned the hard way is that more is not always best.

Here are some questions to help you make an informed decision:

- How does this opportunity align with your long-term career goals and aspirations?
- What new skills, knowledge, or experiences can you gain by taking on this responsibility?
- How will this role enhance your professional reputation or visibility within the organization or industry?
- Will this responsibility allow you to expand your network and connect with influential individuals or mentors?
- What are the potential challenges or risks associated with taking on this additional responsibility, and how can you mitigate them?
- How does this opportunity fit within your current workload and commitments? Can you manage the additional responsibility effectively?
- How does this responsibility align with your values and interests? Will it provide you with a sense of fulfillment and satisfaction in your work?
- How does the expanded responsibility support your *Now, Near, Next*?

By asking these questions and reflecting on the answers, you can better assess whether taking on the additional responsibility will contribute to your professional growth. Consider discussing your thoughts with mentors, a coach, trusted colleagues, or leaders who can provide valuable insights and guidance.

Declining a Stretch Assignment

When the answers to the questions above reveal that the task or job expansion will deliver more volume and less value, how do you say no? I have found the following approaches to work well:

- Offer what you *can* do before stating what you *can't* do. Example: *I would be honored to take on the oversight of that function on a ninety-day interim basis; given my current workload, I would not have the capacity to take that on permanently.*
- Share your perception of the volume-versus-value perception. Example: I had an incredibly talented and ambitious leader who worked for me. She was often volunteering to take on more. As I was considering reorganizing the human resources department, I explored the idea of moving one of the functions under her span of care. To my surprise, she shared that she did not see the natural connection to her other areas of responsibility, and it seemed like a layering of added work without increased value. I was both shocked and impressed. She clarified that she didn't want more, just to have a bigger team.

Widen Your View

Serving externally can be an excellent way to broaden your perspective and build your community of supporters. Depending on your availability, choose a commitment that is right for you so you can lean in unapologetically and guilt-free. Two ways to get involved are volunteering and board service.

Volunteer in an Area of Interest

An effective way for you to gain exposure, broaden your horizon, and meet others is through volunteer service. To begin:

- Identify a cause that is meaningful to you and is aligned with your *Next.*

- Research organizations that support your area of interest.
- Reach out to share your potential interest.
- Choose when, where, and how often you will serve.
- Do not overcommit, as you will add stress or make a poor impression.

Some of the most impactful opportunities in my career began with serving as a volunteer on a committee. With a passion for elevating professional women, I was drawn to the work of the YWCA-St. Louis. After having participated in their leader luncheons for the past few years, I was invited to chair the events committee. Not only did the role provide me an opportunity to give back to an impactful organization, but it also exposed me to several professional women across industries. My network of influential, like-minded women grew exponentially.

Another volunteer assignment led to one of my most proud board appointments. I was blessed to serve on the Catholic Health Association (CHA) of America's CEO search committee a few years ago. That process exposed me to various talented health-care executives and the incredible CHA staff, which ultimately resulted in my candidacy for a board seat.

Assume a Board Appointment

Serving on a board of directors can offer tremendous opportunities for growth and development. If you haven't previously served on a board, starting with a nonprofit board is an excellent grounding. Hospitals, foundations, schools, and associations can be good places to begin.

Board service does not need to be in an area of industry expertise. Identifying your portable talent, skills, and experiences outside of the industry can be an impactful way to broaden your thinking and apply your gifts. The benefits can be plentiful, including:

Influence and Decision-Making: Board members can shape the strategic direction and decision-making processes. You can contribute to important decisions that impact the company's mission, goals, policies, and overall direction.

Networking and Connections: Serving on a board expands your professional network and builds valuable connections. Board members can often interact with other influential leaders, industry experts, and professionals, leading to new opportunities, partnerships, and collaborations.

Skill Development and Learning: Being part of a board provides an opportunity for personal and professional growth. You can enhance your leadership, decision-making, strategic thinking, and problem-solving skills through active participation and exposure to diverse perspectives.

Impact and Giving Back: Serving on a board allows you to make a meaningful impact on the organization and the community it serves. It provides an avenue to give back by contributing time, talent, and treasure to a cause or mission you care about.

Professional Reputation: Serving on a board can enhance your professional reputation and credibility. Being associated with a respected organization and demonstrating a commitment to governance and leadership can positively impact career prospects and opportunities.

Learning from Peers: Being part of a board means working alongside other experienced and knowledgeable individuals. Board members can learn from each other's expertise, experiences, and perspectives, fostering personal and professional growth.

When you are ready, here are some helpful tips:

- Keep in mind that board service comes with tremendous responsibility. Ensuring you have the time and capacity to take on a governance role will be important.

- Prepare yourself by participating in board webinars, courses, publications, and videos. Governance is not the same as management. It is important to know the difference and have a clear understanding of your role and responsibilities as a board member.

- Create a board bio that outlines your core competencies. Boards seek to find diversity of background, experiences, and skill sets. Consider the types of board committees and where your talent and skills may be most valuable, e.g., finance committee, audit committee, or consumer experience committee.

- Reach out to your sponsors and network to share your interest in board appointments. Equip them with your board bio so that they can forward it on your behalf.

- You should carefully consider the expectations, commitments, and specific requirements of the board you are considering joining before committing. It is helpful to request a copy of the charter as well as the member roles and responsibilities document. Bear in mind that some nonprofit boards have an expectation of a philanthropic commitment.

 Ignite Intentionality:

What is one way you will broaden your perspective in the *Now* (stretch internally) and in the *Near* (widen view externally)?

Conclusion

You may have limited knowledge and understanding of different ideas, cultures, beliefs, and experiences when you have a narrow perspective. By broadening your perspective, you expose yourself to diverse viewpoints and gain a deeper understanding of the world and its complexities.

Broadening your perspective enhances intellectual and emotional growth, improves decision-making, fosters inclusivity and empathy, and promotes creativity and innovation. It is an essential aspect of personal development.

Self-advocating, networking, and stepping into new roles may feel like stretching beyond your comfort zone. If you began to feel overwhelmed or insecure at any point in section two, congratulations, you are pushing and challenging yourself. You're probably not doing it right if you aren't a little uncomfortable. Don't worry; we've got you. Chapter seven addresses practical ways to overcome self-doubt, infuse positive self-talk, and show up.

Reflection: Broaden Your Perspective

Penny Pennington is the managing partner of Edward Jones, a leading financial services company dedicated to helping its 8 million clients turn their life plans into financial plans. Under her leadership, the firm delivers on its purpose to partner for positive impact, improve the lives of its clients and colleagues, and improve its communities and society.

I worked in corporate banking for fourteen years at the start of my career, and while I learned a lot and was successful, I knew I needed something different. It was important to me that it was me showing up to work every day and applying my skills, gifts, and ambitions to make a difference. I didn't have the word for it then, but now I do—I wanted to *thrive* in my career and fulfill my purpose.

Early on in my career, I certainly didn't imagine that I would someday be the managing partner of Edward Jones. But I like to think that I put myself in a position to succeed by being a lifelong learner and learning to always say "yes" to opportunities that would allow me to make a real impact.

That wasn't always the case. There were times when I wasn't as bold as my instincts told me to be and times when I didn't always raise my hand for opportunities when I thought I wasn't 100 percent qualified for them. Over time, I learned that I can deliver more value to the firm and to all whom we serve when I'm my full self and bring who I am to the picture. I also learned to trust in my capabilities and know that I can learn the technical aspects of any role once I'm in it. Those mindsets helped prepare me for success in many of the roles I've held throughout my career. Someone gave me a great insight about leaning into new experiences—you may not be fully qualified.

The same advice we give to clients applies to our careers: be prepared and build resilience into your approach. If an opportunity comes along that wasn't expected but offers the potential to make a real impact, be ready to say yes to it. Learn as much as you can. Ask a lot of questions. Be curious. Being a lifelong learner helps to build that resiliency into your career and not only helps you to be ready for opportunities but also gives you the confidence to take on roles that might make you nervous initially.

I'll share the advice someone gave me years ago, which I apply almost every day in my role: Get comfortable with being uncomfortable. Stretch your boundaries. Be bold, believe in yourself, and take on the opportunities that make you nervous or even scare you. Have faith in your abilities and that you'll learn the technical details of a role once you're in it. Keep raising your hand and keep saying yes.

Section Two: Near—Ignite Intentionality

Take a moment to consider all the ways we have addressed igniting intentionality in section two. Pause to revisit the personal reflections. How will you remain mindful of the key learnings? Using the *Now, Near, Next* Companion Guide, or a journal, check to ensure you have documented all the quick action steps and created accountability for yourself. Lastly, charting your *Now, Near, Next Blueprint* is in full swing. Take time to crystalize your thoughts. We will continue to loop back to your plan throughout section three.

 Personal Reflection

 Take Quick Action

 Chart in *Now, Near, Next Blueprint*

Chapter Four:

▲ What is your *Next*?

☁ How much time will you realistically, unapologetically commit to your growth in the *Now*?

☁ To what degree does your current role allow you to consistently exercise your natural gifts and talents?

☁ When would you like the transition to your *Next* to occur?

▲ Based on your *Next* target date, take a moment to document the start date of your *Now* (today's date) and the start date of your *Near* (two-thirds of the time before your *Next*). Include this date on your *Now, Near, Next Blueprint*.

➤ Document on your *Now, Near, Next Blueprint* some of the preliminary action items that you will focus on in the *Now*.

➤ Document a minimum of one strength-development goal to focus on in your *Now* and your *Near*.

☁ What new behavior do you wish to amplify? What old behavior will you choose to diminish?

➤ Develop your elevator speech.

Chapter Five:

➤ Document your Life's Board of Directors and commit to contacting at least one.

▲ Who are the people in your organization, industry, or community who could positively influence your *Next*?

➤ Identify one Sponsor whom you will share your aspirations with.

▲ Choose one way you will expand your network in your *Now* and one way you will expand your network in your *Near*.

Chapter Six:

🔺 What would be one way to broaden your perspective in your *Now* and your *Near*?

SECTION THREE

Next—Actualize Potential

"Section Three: Next—Actualize Potential" addresses both walking with confidence and having the courage to spread your wings. A Next, by definition, has some elements of the unknown. Having a plan while leaving room for life's unexpected twists and turns allows you to be agile and maximize opportunities.

CHAPTER SEVEN

Radiate Confidence

It's not your job to like me; it's mine.

— **Byron Katie,** American spiritual writer

Twenty-five-plus years ago, I was on assignment as the facilitator of an "executive and board presentation skills course" for an external client. Now, if you are doing the math, you can appreciate that I was in my late twenties. When the participants began to arrive, I was a bit surprised and a tad intimidated. What sat before me were twelve fifty- to sixty-year-old men.

I stood in my skirt suit and closed-toed shoes, prepared to teach these "old dogs" new tricks. Some sat with arms folded; others resorted to charm, and the remainder seemed slightly intrigued with what the course may have to offer.

I recall my mind racing and self-doubt creeping in. "I'm sure they are wondering what I have to teach them. I bet they think this is a waste of time. How am I going to convince these men that I have the talent, skills, and experience despite my relative youth?"

Admittedly, I recall starting a little weakly. The blank stares were almost as daunting as the looks of annoyance. As is often the case when I get overcome with nerves, it goes straight to my stomach. Time in the ladies' room, cold water, a fresh lip, and a lot of positive self-talk—I was ready to go.

By channeling that nervous energy into self-affirming statements, the playing field was somewhat leveled. As I leaned into my talents and deep subject-matter expertise, the old dudes walked away with new skills and increased respect for what this twentysomething had to offer.

Transitions to your *Next* will mean performing in new areas. As you broaden your perspective and amplify your aspirations, you may find moments where you feel over your skis. Acknowledging when self-doubt is holding you back, instituting and reinforcing positive self-talk, and being present are instrumental in building and exercising confidence.

Throughout this chapter, we will provide insight into the basis and benefits of self-efficacy, a practical tool to generate positive energy, and evidence-based guidance on being present. Whether you are naturally confident, with only occasional uncertainty, or feeling a bit insecure about where we've pushed you thus far, you've got this!

Embolden Self-Efficacy

As women, we don't allow ourselves to think we deserve more. And when we don't deserve more, we tend to allow ourselves to stay in situations that make us complacent.

— **Tiffany Owens,** Vice President, Human Resources

Impostor Syndrome

Also known as impostor phenomenon or fraud syndrome.

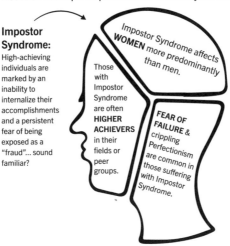

Impostor Syndrome: High-achieving individuals are marked by an inability to internalize their accomplishments and a persistent fear of being exposed as a "fraud"... sound familiar?

Those with Impostor Syndrome are often **HIGHER ACHIEVERS** in their fields or peer groups.

Impostor Syndrome affects **WOMEN** more predominantly than men.

FEAR OF FAILURE & crippling Perfectionism are common in those suffering with Impostor Syndrome.

Kris Windley (withakwriting.com)

Self-efficacy is a concept developed by psychologist Albert Bandura and refers to an individual's belief in their ability to succeed in specific situations or accomplish specific tasks. It plays a crucial role in personal development, motivation, and achievement. Regarding women, self-efficacy holds particular importance due to the unique societal and cultural factors that can influence their experiences. The sad truth is that up to 82 percent of people face feelings of imposter syndrome, a sense that they haven't earned what they have achieved and are a fraud (Bravata, 2020). These feelings can contribute to increased anxiety and depression, less career risk-taking, and career burnout. If your perceptions are "I am not qualified enough, I am not competent enough, I am not good enough, I am not smart enough," that mental model and internal narrative will shape your actions and behaviors. Why would you apply, try, and put your interest out there? We can become paralyzed by our self-doubt.

Symptoms of imposter syndrome include:

- Crediting luck or other reasons for any success.
- Fear of being seen as a failure.
- Feeling that overworking is the only way to meet expectations.
- Feeling unworthy of attention or affection.
- Downplaying accomplishments.
- Holding back from reaching attainable goals.

Building self-efficacy is a gradual process that involves developing confidence in your abilities and belief in your potential. As I consider my *Next*, I find myself questioning if I have what it takes, wondering if I can make it on my own. We have shared many strategies throughout the book, which I am working to adopt, and will continue revealing additional techniques.

Practice Self-Reflection (Chapter Three): Engage in regular self-reflection to gain insight into your strengths, areas for improvement, and personal growth. Reflecting on your past successes and how you overcame challenges can reinforce your belief in your abilities and boost your self-efficacy.

As I consider a career dedicated to supporting women through coaching, education, public speaking, and writing, I'm reflecting on my talent spotlight and the impact that I've made thus far.

Set Realistic Goals (Chapter Four): Start by setting realistic and achievable goals that you can unapologetically, without guilt, commit to. Break them down into smaller, manageable steps that you can work on. Accomplishing these goals will provide evidence of your capabilities and build your confidence.

Putting my *Now, Near, Next* in writing and formulating a timeline has made the journey feel more manageable and helped build my confidence.

Develop Competence (Chapters Four–Six): Acquire and enhance the skills necessary for your desired goals. Take courses, seek mentorship, or engage in activities that allow you to develop expertise in areas relevant to your aspirations. The more competent you feel, the stronger your self-efficacy will become.

Completing my executive coaching certification and passing the board certification definitely boosted my confidence.

Seek Positive Role Models (Chapter Five): Surround yourself with positive role models who embody the qualities and skills you aspire to develop. Observe and learn from their experiences and use their success stories to inspire your journey.

Walking this path with Kimberly K. Rath has provided me the mentoring and encouragement to stay the course.

Take on Challenges (Chapters Six and Eight): Step out of your comfort zone and take on new challenges. Embrace opportunities that push you to learn and grow. As you successfully navigate challenging situations, your belief in your abilities will strengthen. More on this in chapter eight.

Taking on authoring this book, a dream of twenty years, is definitely empowering.

Coming in Chapter Nine...

Spoiler alert: I had to spend a fair amount of time in chapter nine. Stay tuned.

Learn from Failure: Embrace failure as an opportunity for growth and learning. View setbacks as temporary and use them as valuable lessons to improve your skills and strategies. Resilience in the face of failure can enhance your self-efficacy.

Take Care of Yourself: Prioritize self-care and maintain physical and mental well-being. Engage in activities that promote relaxation, reduce stress, and boost confidence. Taking care of yourself holistically contributes to a positive self-image and strengthens self-efficacy.

Celebrate Small Victories: Acknowledge and celebrate your achievements no matter how small they may seem. Recognizing your progress and accomplishments will reinforce your belief in your abilities and motivate you to strive for success.

 Actualize Potential:

Where do you need to place additional focus to further develop self-efficacy?

As we will continue to unpack in this chapter, one of the most proven ways to grow self-efficacy is to challenge negative self-talk. Replacing negative thoughts with positive and affirming statements will impact your behavior, performance, and confidence.

Practice Positive Self-Talk

Talk to yourself like you would to someone you love.

— **Brené Brown,** American professor and author

Mayo Clinic researchers suggest that positive self-talk is linked to numerous health and well-being benefits, including:

- Increased life span
- Lower rates of depression
- Lower levels of distress and pain

- Greater resistance to illnesses
- Better psychological and physical well-being
- Better cardiovascular health and reduced risk of death from cardiovascular disease and stroke
- Reduced risk of death from cancer
- Reduced risk of death from respiratory conditions
- Reduced risk of death from infections
- Better coping skills during hardships and times of stress

In theory, it makes sense that positive inner dialogue would have natural health benefits. However, behavioral science and positive psychology have revealed that positivity doesn't come naturally for everyone. If you have positivity in your top five talent themes, you may struggle less with reversing negative self-talk. For others, it takes more effort.

Let's imagine that your boss stops by your office. She leans in and says, "Can I speak to you for a moment?" You begin to worry as you gather your tablet and walk to her office. "I wonder what this is about? I bet she didn't like that report I submitted. I bet she's unhappy about my comment in yesterday's meeting. Great! This is just what I needed on a Monday!"

What you tell yourself, that internal voice that questions, catastrophizes, doubts, and worries, significantly impacts whether you will get moving or stay still. Your perceptions influence your internal narrative and, if not edited, impact your behavior. Instead, nullify negative self-talk as follows:

Pause:

When you realize that you are going down that path, interrupt the negative thought and hit a hard pause.

I wonder what this is about? I bet she didn't like that report I submitted. STOP.

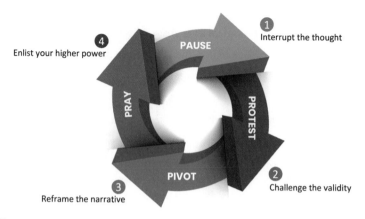

1 Interrupt the thought
PAUSE
4 Enlist your higher power
PRAY
PROTEST
2 Challenge the validity
PIVOT
3 Reframe the narrative

Protest:

Challenge the validity of the thought, cross-examine the idea, and recognize the lack of hard evidence you have to support it.

There is no evidence or rationale to assume this is negative. Making assumptions is dangerous and does not prepare me to be at my best.

Pivot:

Change the narrative to a positive expression. University of Michigan psychologist Ethan Kross's research found that "I" is often used in framing these negative thoughts. However, when a person uses their first name, they are more likely to develop a positive expression: "Linda, you can do this."

Maybe she has positive feedback, a new assignment, or an idea to consider. Linda, whatever it is, you've got this!

Pray:

Whatever your faith tradition, seeking guidance, wisdom, and strength from your higher power, the universe, or within can help release negative energy and replace it with a sense of peace.

Give me strength, confidence, ears to hear, and wisdom to speak.

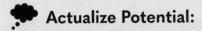

Actualize Potential:

What affirming statement can you incorporate into your self-talk to promote positivity and momentum in your life?

Assume Positive Intent

Your beliefs become your thoughts, your thoughts become your words, your words become your actions, your actions become your habits, your habits become your values, your values become your destiny.

— **Mahatma Gandhi,** political and spiritual leader

In addition to controlling our narrative, we can generate or stagnate energy by how we think of others. It is so easy to jump to the wrong conclusion, particularly in this age of technology. Emails, texts, tweets, and various written formats have only exacerbated this issue, leaving the interpretation of tone and intention to the receiver. Depending on our self-talk, mood, circumstances, etc., we may not read a message as the sender intended.

Assuming positive intent has been a mantra in my leadership dialogue. If a message strikes a nerve, try reading it in a different tone, give grace to the sender, who may have been rushed or having a tough day, and do not presume that the intention was negative and directed at you. In cases where you cannot identify a positive meaning, reach out to the sender. In the spirit of the right relationship, you can inquire where the other person is coming from and, if appropriate, address how the message felt.

This is another excellent place to apply Pause, Protest, Pivot, and Pray. Much time can be wasted ruminating, filling in blanks, and building a counterattack. Relationships and credibility are damaged when there is an assumption of negative intention, and an overreaction or defensive posturing ensues. The premise of positive intent will keep you moving forward with positive velocity.

Show Up and Speak Up

No matter how you feel, get up, dress up, and show up.

— **Regina Brett,** American journalist

In studying the subject of confidence and self-empowerment, I had an ah-ha moment. There was a period of time when many of the long-tenured executive team worked from home, and our leader at the time worked from another state. We managed most of our meetings through virtual platforms and stayed connected electronically. I was a machine. I worked even crazier hours than before, cranking out quality and finding creative ways to engage my remote teams. Frankly, I loved it.

When our former leader retired and a successor was appointed, he promoted several people to the executive team. He became my new boss, and I had several new peers.

Although many of us continued to work off-site, my new leader and many of my predominantly male counterparts began to come into the office on a regular basis. I continued to work tirelessly from home, measuring my value by time, outcomes, and performance. My interactions with the executive were regularly online and occasionally in person.

In hindsight, I failed to appreciate that I was unknowingly diminishing my value among some members of the new team by being less visible. They placed importance on being together in person, getting in early and staying late. I placed importance on connecting with my team, beginning my day early, and delivering results. There is no right or wrong. However, this became another valuable lesson in intentionality. I had to be more purposeful about developing those relationships.

Even in this digital age, Coleman's 1996 theory on empowerment still holds true almost thirty years later. Leaders get noticed and promoted based on exposure (60 percent) and image (30 percent) over performance (10 percent). Yet women like me massively over-index on performance. Visibility trumps performance every time.

Be Seen

I have found luck is quite predictable. If you want more luck, take more chances. Be more active. Show up more often.

— **Bryan Tracy,** Canadian-American motivational speaker and author

Here is the conundrum. While the research by Gartner (2021) shows that remote employees perform as much as 5 percent better than those in the office, 64 percent of managers still believe that in-office workers are higher-performing and more likely to give them a larger merit increase. In addition, compared to men, women knowledge workers have a stronger desire to work remotely. As such, without intentionality, more women will be working remotely or hybrid, performing excellently, and being passed up for higher salaries and promotions than their male counterparts who choose to work in the office.

Whether we like it or not, showing up and being present is still essential in many organizations. As we reviewed in chapter four regarding culture fit, it is important to understand the corporate culture and your leader's expectations. I still hear executives assess an employee's dedication with statements like, "She was always in the office before me and left after me." Consider your priorities, the days and times most critical to be in person, and advocate for a schedule that accommodates the balance you need.

Showing up doesn't necessarily mean you must be in the office every day for ten hours; however, when you are in the office, be present. Use this time to schedule in-person meetings, leave open time on your calendar for informal connections, and avoid meetings that have you behind closed doors all day. Take time to walk around the halls to check in with colleagues and team members. Be seen.

As much as I enjoyed the convenience of working from home and the productivity I gained, I realized I was missing essential relationship-building. Shifting back to going into the office, I have preserved Friday as a day I routinely work from home. With a team in multiple states, I schedule all my video conferences for Friday. If I'm going to sit in an office all day on the computer, I may as well do so without shoes.

Here are a few additional reasons why in-person time is valuable:

Collaboration and Teamwork: In-person interactions can foster better collaboration and teamwork among colleagues. Being physically present allows for spontaneous discussions, brainstorming sessions, and face-to-face communication, enhancing creativity, problem-solving, and innovation.

Relationship-Building: Being in the office provides opportunities for building stronger relationships with coworkers and leaders. Informal conversations, social interactions, and networking events can help establish connections, trust, and rapport, which can benefit career growth and professional development.

Mentorship and Learning: Being physically present in the office can facilitate mentorship and learning opportunities. Observing and learning from experienced colleagues, participating in training sessions, and engaging in professional development activities can enhance skills and knowledge.

Company Culture and Engagement: Being present in the office can contribute to a sense of belonging and engagement with the company's culture. Participating in team-building activities, attending company-wide meetings, and experiencing the office environment firsthand can help employees align with the organization's values and goals.

In addition to showing up and being present, how you engage is critical. Women bring diverse perspectives, experiences, and ideas to the table. By speaking up, you ensure that your unique viewpoints are considered. This leads to better decision-making and problem-solving, as diverse perspectives foster innovation and creativity.

 Actualize Potential:

In what ways do you need to show up more intentionally?

Be Heard

When I dare to be powerful, to use my strength in the service of my vision, then it becomes less and less important whether I am afraid.

— **Audre Lorde,** American writer and civil rights activist

Unfortunately, women often face societal pressure to be accommodating and polite and avoid appearing overly assertive or aggressive. As a result, they may use qualifiers to soften their statements or appear less confrontational. This behavior stems from seeking to navigate gender norms and avoid backlash or negative reactions.

I recently recognized a qualifier I often use among my male peers: "This may be a naïve question, but..." I suppose I say that to minimize the embarrassment that may ensue if it is, in fact, a silly question. In doing so, I minimize whatever it is I'm questioning.

There are women I hear routinely apologizing for speaking up, offering differing opinions, or asking for something to be repeated. I suspect these habits are unintentional yet deeply conditioned for many of us. To avoid unintentionally invalidating your communication, remember certain words and phrases that can undermine your message. Here are some language patterns to avoid:

Minimizing language: Steer clear of language that downplays or diminishes the importance or impact of your statements. For example:

- "I'm just..."
- "This might be a silly question, but..."
- "I'm no expert, but..."
- "Hopefully..."

Apologetic language: Avoid excessive or unnecessary apologies that can diminish your authority or make your statements appear less valid. For instance:

- "I'm sorry, but..."
- "I apologize if this is wrong, but..."

Hedging language: Reduce language that adds uncertainty or doubt to your statements. Instead, aim for more assertive and confident expressions. For instance, avoid:

- "I think" or "I believe" (when stating a fact)
- "Maybe" or "perhaps" (when you have a strong opinion or knowledge)
- "Sort of" or "kind of" (when describing something specific)

Disclaimers: Avoid excessive disclaimers that can weaken your statements before expressing them. While some disclaimers may be necessary, try to use them sparingly. For example, omit:

- "I'm not sure if this is right, but..."
- "I may be wrong, but..."

Tag questions: Be mindful of using them excessively, as they can diminish the authority and assertiveness of your statements. For example:

- "Don't you think?"
- "Isn't it?"
- "Would you agree?"

Overusing qualifiers: Limit excessive qualifiers that can weaken the strength of your statements. Instead, use qualifiers selectively and intentionally. For instance:

- "I could be wrong, but..."
- "It's just my opinion, but..."

By being conscious of these language patterns and striving to use more direct, confident, and assertive language, you can communicate your thoughts and ideas more effectively and ensure your messages are received with the weight they deserve. It can be helpful to enlist the support of someone you trust. Invite them to privately point out to you when you use words or phrases that dilute or minimize your message.

 Actualize Potential:

What common word or phrase must you remove from your communication style?

Instead, use strong, assertive language to validate your statements and convey confidence. Here are some words and phrases that can enhance the strength of your message:

- "I am confident..."
- "I strongly believe..."
- "I have evidence/research/data to support my statement..."
- "Based on my experience/expertise, I can say..."
- "I am certain..."
- "I am convinced..."
- "It is clear/evident/apparent..."
- "I assert/assertively state..."
- "I have full faith in my conclusion/decision because..."
- "My analysis/assessment leads me to the firm conclusion..."

Incorporating these words and phrases can help convey conviction and authority in your statements. Remember to pair strong language with the substance and validity of your arguments or evidence. Confidence comes from your words and the strength of your knowledge, preparation, and delivery.

Be Brief, Be Bold, Be Brilliant

Several months ago, a colleague and trusted friend offered me constructive advice. He suggested that instead of facilitating a discussion on topics I brought forward in our executive meetings, I should come with an expert opinion and assumptive close. He suggested that all decisions do not require a democratic approach and consensus. As the subject-matter expert in my field, he felt I needed to assert a stronger approach.

I found this somewhat countercultural and counterintuitive yet empowering. The challenge was rewiring my approach and putting that advice into action.

There have been instances where professional women have faced backlash when they were perceived as coming on too strong or assertively. This phenomenon is often called the "backlash effect" or the "double bind." It stems from societal expectations and gender biases that can penalize women for exhibiting assertiveness or displaying behaviors typically associated with men in leadership.

An article by Heath, Flynn, and Holt (2014) offered valuable and still-relevant insight into how men perceive women in the proverbial boardroom. In general, there remains a Venus-Mars conundrum when it comes to communication among genders.

HE SAID SHE SAID

HE SAID	SHE SAID
We're afraid of how women will react to criticism.	We don't get feedback, even when we ask for it.
Women need to be concise and remain on point.	We don't like to repackage old ideas or restate the obvious.
Women need a stronger point of view.	It's difficult to get a word in.
Women need to speak informally and off-the-cuff.	We like to put together presentations.
Women get defensive when they are challenged.	We obsess about a meeting for days after it's over.
Women are more emotional than men.	It's not emotion—it's passion.
Women are less confident than men.	Yes, but we're outnumbered five to one, and we tend to feel less fully "at the table."

(Heath, Flynn, and Holt, 2014)

As women find their voice, they are often challenged with balancing their natural facilitative, collaborative approach with a more directive, assertive style. The *HBR* article and our qualitative research offer the following suggestions:

Be Brief: Research suggests that women are generally more animated and expressive than men. In general, it is suggested that women use more words to make a point or tell a story. They include more detail, at times unnecessary, and incorporate more "feeling words."

My personal experience would suggest this is more stylistic than gender-based, particularly among individuals that have a strong passion for highly technical subjects. Nevertheless, brevity is a worthy skill to develop. When bringing an opinion or idea to the discussion, keep in mind tone, inflection, and facts. Getting to the point without unnecessary commentary is essential to engaging your audience. It is OK to be passionate, provided your enthusiasm is balanced with data to support your perspective, and the point is not lost in the delivery.

Be Bold: Research suggests that men are more inclined to show up early or stay after a meeting for the informal discussion. Women tend to show up on time and rush to their next meeting. I can attest to this as my reality, and it relates back to being seen. You can't have an effective pre-meeting on Zoom.

There is much to be said for counting your votes in advance and investing in the relationships. If the casual watercooler conversations or pre-meeting discussions aren't possible, set up time in advance of the meeting with a few participants. Pitch your idea, solicit their feedback, and ask for their support in the meeting. I find that the pre-meeting is most advantageous when you gain support from those that you expect to have the most questions or pushback.

Be Brilliant: Many women prefer to bring a thoughtful presentation. We are generally more comfortable, more succinct, and more persuasive when we have packaged our remarks. Research suggests that men are more inclined to think out loud, debate a topic, and reach a conclusion after impromptu discussion.

Here are some ways to prepare to contribute spontaneously—yes, an oxymoron.

1. If there are any pre-read materials, take time to note questions or thoughts that you have related to the topic.
2. If the discussion comes up without advanced information, jot down questions, thoughts, and ideas as they come to you and bring forth your comment using the confidence framing described in the prior section.

3. Show up prepared to participate. Walk into meetings with the mental preparation to be present, take notes, and contribute. Set the intention in advance.

Conclusion

Self-efficacy, fostering positive self-talk, showing up, and speaking up are all essential to radiating confidence. When you are confident, you are more likely to take on challenges, pursue your goals, and make decisions without second-guessing yourself. It helps you recognize your worth, skills, and accomplishments, leading to a sense of empowerment.

Without self-confidence, you are more likely to pass up or miss opportunities. Having a foundation of confidence will be critical as we move to risk-taking. Reflect on your self-efficacy and practice the concepts outlined in chapter eight before moving to chapter nine. When you are ready, buckle up. We're getting off the merry-go-round and headed for Splash Mountain!

Reflection: Radiate Confidence

Stop pretending to be something you're not. It is unsustainable and exhausting, and you never truly know if you have been embraced for the real you or the fake you.

— **Nina Blackshear,** JD, corporate attorney and certified executive coach

Nina Blackshear is a corporate attorney and certified executive coach. She has pivoted several times, working in major gift fundraising, marketing communications, human resources, and real estate. Though her coaching practice is inclusive, she is passionate about offering a safe space for successful women (particularly women of color) to overcome limiting beliefs, lead with confidence, and level up to "What's Next."

Nina earned her BA in Political and Social Thought from the University of Virginia and her JD from the University of Virginia School of Law. She holds a graduate certificate in Strategic Communication and Cross-Cultural Leadership from Temple University's Klein College of Media and Communication.

Nina is a board member of the Association of Corporate Counsel (Greater Philadelphia Chapter). She is on the advisory board of CenterForce USA, which holds diversity conferences and workshops designed for the legal profession around the country. She provides executive and leadership coaching to senior-level and C-Suite clients across industries. She is regularly sought out to weigh in on various legal and leadership topics for webinars, podcasts, and conferences.

Nina lives in the Philadelphia area with her husband and one too many cats.

"If you feel like an imposter, it might be because you are one." Well, that certainly got everyone's attention.

I spoke to a room full of women, most of them successful

corporate attorneys. And as it inevitably does when high-achieving women gather, imposter syndrome had entered the conversation. Throughout the day, attendees had been 78 percent paying attention and 22 percent covertly checking their phones or half-opened laptops to keep on top of emails. But when I uttered this statement, all eyes turned toward the front of the room.

I often make this statement when speaking, particularly to successful women, for two reasons: One, it is generally a novel and slightly controversial concept for most who hear it, and two, it is (at least partially) true. More on that in a moment.

A friend once told me that my level of confidence was almost sociopathic. I think what reads as "confidence" is simply me being comfortable in my skin and with the person I've become.

But it hasn't always been that way.

For much of my life, I felt like an imposter or, at the very least, an outsider. Here are a few examples:

- I look different from most of my immediate and extended family members.
- From kindergarten through fifth grade, I attended an exclusive and predominantly white private school as one of the few black children—my classmates knew (or assumed) I was receiving some measure of "financial support."
- We moved during my sophomore year of high school, and I never really found my footing with a close group of friends in my new environment.
- I went to law school because I wasn't sure what else to do after college, and while there, I felt like an alien from outer space who didn't speak or understand this strange new language—or the social nuances that accompanied attending an elite law school in the South.
- I've pivoted through many careers and industries, including

law, real estate, human resources, pharmaceutical marketing and communications, higher education fundraising, and back to law. Sure, all that "jungle gym" skill-gathering serves me wonderfully now, but it has also meant I've never quite felt at home in any of my roles.

I list those experiences to illustrate that different circumstances may make us feel like we don't belong—like imposters who will be promptly shown the door once everyone figures out that we shouldn't have been let in in the first place. That is externally driven imposter syndrome, and the bad news is that we may be unable to do much about those factors. We can stand up for ourselves, set boundaries, establish what we will or won't tolerate, and exit a situation. But it is not completely within our control to change things.

Then there is the other kind of imposter syndrome. The kind I am addressing when I drop my "You may be an imposter" bomb on unsuspecting conference attendees. And that is internally driven imposter syndrome. It is just as harmful as externally driven imposter syndrome, but this one comes with a silver lining: it is nearly 100 percent within your control to manage and eliminate it.

I'm not trying to actualize their deep-seated fears when I tell women they may be imposters. But I am trying to get them to realize the part they may play in setting themselves up to feel like frauds, outsiders, cheats, etc. Because if a woman pretends to be something she is not, know something she does not know, believe something she does not believe, or want something she does not want because she thinks that is how she will be "successful" in each environment, culture, or relationship, then she is complicit in her imposter syndrome.

This is especially true of highly successful women who are used to being in the top tier of their class, on the winning team, or recognized for their achievements. They have become so used to being perceived as winners and experts that admitting that they don't know something or don't have it "all figured out" becomes repellent.

And after a while, it becomes terrifying.

Because if they're not the winner with all the answers when a question is asked—who the heck are they?

Women must learn to stop participating in their imposter-syndrome misery. The patriarchy, microaggressions, misogyny, glass ceilings, and glass cliffs probably aren't going anywhere soon. But women's ability to push back against the onslaught of externally driven imposter syndrome is considerably hampered if they are feeding the internally driven imposter-syndrome monster with every minor misrepresentation, piece of puffery, and "fake it till you make it" fallacy.

If I could pass on lessons that I've learned over the years that have served me well and been critical to eliminating my imposter syndrome, they would be these:

Stop pretending to be something you're not. It is unsustainable and exhausting, and you never truly know if you have been embraced for the real you or the fake you. That's an incredibly lonely feeling.

Get comfortable with these three words: "I don't know." This tip is initially uncomfortable for high achievers but so liberating once you get the hang of it. Unless you really should know (like, it's a core function of your job), generally, nothing will burn to the ground if you tell someone you need to investigate something and get back to them. However, I have seen things crumble to ashes when someone answered a question inaccurately because they felt pressured to look like an "expert on the spot," and others relied on that information to drive their own decisions.

Finally, just because a situation is unfamiliar to you doesn't mean you don't belong there. Every situation is unfamiliar—until it's not. Look to your past for all the evidence you could require.

Get granular to unearth dozens of examples of circumstances that felt alien to you until you got into a groove that eventually became a rhythm so seamless you don't even notice it anymore. Whatever is "next" for you will be the same. I promise.

CHAPTER EIGHT

Take Risks

*Get out of your comfort zone, prove yourself wrong, and if it
does not work out, then it's "oh well,"
but just keep moving forward.*

— **Jenny Svoboda,** entrepreneur

Let's face it: taking risks is relative to where you are.
In my early twenties, I had an opportunity within my company that
required a move from San Diego to Orange County. My greatest
fear was finding an apartment that would allow dogs. That seems
silly compared to considering a move with school-age children
to Las Vegas or another move across the country for a job in an
industry where I had no prior experience.

Over my thirty-year career, I have worked for five amazing
organizations. Three of the five opportunities came to me when
I was not looking. In every case, I was hesitant to respond to
the invitation to interview and nearly talked myself out of the
opportunity before saying yes. Fear of the unknown and comfort in
the known would initially convince me to stay put. Fortunately, my

supporters were available to offer the advice and encouragement I needed to harness my fear and make bold moves.

Taking risks requires being open to change. The more adaptable you are, the greater your opportunity to strengthen your essentiality and relevance. Chapter eight moves you to channel your emboldened self-confidence into advancing professional skills and knowledge and taking calculated risks.

Harness Your Fear

Don't be afraid. Be focused. Be determined. Be hopeful. Be empowered.

— **Michelle Obama,** American attorney, author, former First Lady of the United States

For thirty years, I have been either the primary or the sole breadwinner. I have had corporate positions that afforded me a consistent biweekly paycheck, health benefits, and paid time off. While there are no guarantees, by working hard and delivering results, I have felt some control over my financial security. My *Next*, however, will put all of that at risk. It's a little scary.

As you consider your *Next*, it is important that you assess the degree of change and extent of adaptability that will be required. Advancing in your current organization may invite less change than considering a new company or industry. Staying in a familiar lane may be easier than stretching into a new core competency. Are you playing it safe or pushing yourself to dream big?

In reviewing your Talent Spotlight, note whether Agility is among your top five talent themes. For those who have strong natural agility, you are energized by change because it provides an opportunity to shift gears. Individuals with softer natural agility may need more time to adjust to change. (Keep in mind, just because a theme is not listed in your top five doesn't mean it isn't a natural talent; it could be your sixth-strongest theme.)

Even among those who are naturally adaptable, change can elicit fear. The most common reasons we avoid or pursue opportunities that require change are the following:

Fear of the Unknown: Throughout human history, unknown situations have often presented potential risks or threats. As a result, individuals who were cautious and apprehensive in new or unfamiliar environments were more likely to avoid potential dangers and survive. In the modern experience, apprehension turns into negative self-talk. We justify the safety of the known by imagining the worst-case scenario of what would be new.

Fear of Failure: Whether it stems from perfectionism, self-doubt, or past failures or we place a higher value on avoiding potential losses than acquiring potential gains, fear of failure is paralyzing.

Loss of Control: People have a natural inclination to seek control and predictability in their lives, and when faced with the unknown, this sense of control is disrupted, leading to feelings of fear or anxiety.

All these fears resonate with me as I consider my *Next*. Whatever your *Next* entails, challenge yourself to ensure you are not limiting your aspirations out of fear. Here are some strategies to help you harness change and increase your adaptability:

Challenge Negative Self-Talk: When you begin to imagine all the reasons that a change will result in negative outcomes or that you will fail, then pause, protest, pivot, and pray. You've got this.

Focus on the Benefits of Change: The change you are considering will bring new opportunities, growth, and learning experiences. Remind yourself of the positive outcomes that can arise from taking a risk.

Do Your Homework: Taking a leap of faith with your career should come with safety gear. Research an organization you may be considering, understand fully the role and expectations you may be pursuing, and develop a financial plan for a situation that brings greater volatility. You will feel a greater sense of control, and less will be unknown, if you do your homework.

Prepare: For some, change is an endorphin. For others, it is like a root canal. Your *Now, Near, Next Blueprint* is intended to prepare you for your *Next.* All the work you will do to develop your purpose, invest in your talent, skills, and knowledge, broaden your reach, and enlist supporters will bolster your confidence and adaptability and ready you to embrace the change.

 Actualize Potential:

What is your greatest fear related to your *Next*? What is one thing you could do to harness that energy and mitigate that fear?

Staying in the same place requires extraordinarily little energy. It is easier and more comfortable; it is also self-limiting. Overcoming the fear of the unknown and concerns of failure or loss of control allows you to fully actualize your potential.

Make Bold Moves

If you're brave enough to change your scenery and figure out somewhere else to go land, you might be pleasantly surprised.

— **Nina Blackshear,** JD, corporate attorney and certified executive coach

We have addressed several reasons why women might stay with an employer even while being overlooked for promotional opportunities. Thus far, we have suggested that they may be too busy to look up, lack the confidence to express their aspirations, or feel inadequate or undeserving of advancement. In addition to some of these self-limiting beliefs and behaviors, there is the element of loyalty.

Research suggests that women tend to exhibit higher loyalty to companies than men. Women:

- Demonstrate stronger emotional attachment to their work, colleagues, and the company's mission.
- Are often found to engage in higher levels of organizational citizenship behavior, such as helping colleagues, volunteering for extra tasks, and showing dedication to the company's success.
- Stay with companies that provide supportive environments and flexible arrangements, allowing a balanced approach to their personal and professional lives.

It is important to recognize that making a bold move can happen within your current organization. As an entrepreneur, Kimberly has made numerous bold moves throughout her thirty-five-year career with Talent Plus.® In my twelve years with my current organization, I've had more than one opportunity to advance in an unfamiliar area. That said, staying for the wrong reason or complacency is not actualizing your potential.

Everything we have discussed up to this point will increase the likelihood of opportunities within and outside of your current circumstances arising and being presented to you. With that in mind, here are three vital recommendations:

Keep your résumé/CV up to date: I can't tell you how many women I hear suggest that their résumé is outdated because they aren't looking or haven't been interviewed in years. They say this as a badge of honor and emphasize their loyalty. What it suggests to me is that they either have not made themselves visible for potential opportunities or have not been planful about their future.

If a door opens, listen: I recently received a call from a former colleague requesting a coaching session. His dilemma was that he was being pursued by three organizations for bigger roles, with larger salaries, in the field that was consistent with his *Next*. (Yes, this framework works for men too.) His concern was that he had been at his current organization for only one year.

I asked him, "What do you perceive as the risk of having an exploratory conversation?" He concluded it was premature to worry about leaving his new job. Just because one door opens does not mean you have to walk through it, but you can't evaluate the merits of the opportunity if you haven't explored it.

Do not run from something; run to something: Unless your current organization violates your core values or subjects you to a hostile work environment, you should not jump ship without discernment and finding the right *Next* move. I can't tell you the number of boomerang hires I have had from people who thought they were leaving for greener grass only to find out everyone has weeds. When you are ready to make a bold move, ensure it is for all the right reasons and consistent with the plan for your *Next.*

 Actualize Potential:

How prepared are you to respond to a job solicitation or to actively pursue an opportunity of interest? What do you need to do to increase your readiness?

Ultimately, taking risks and making bold moves in business can empower you by allowing you to step out of your comfort zone and push your limits. It helps build confidence, assertiveness, and resilience, which are crucial for success in any field.

Foster a Growth Mindset

I'd rather regret the risks that didn't work out than the chances I didn't take at all.

— **Simone Biles,** American gymnast

One of the most difficult conversations for a leader is informing someone that the company has decided to terminate employment. These conversations are even more heartbreaking when the employee has dedicated their professional life to the company and is a wonderful culture fit. Still, their skills, knowledge, and talents have not developed with the pace of change. Mid-career spans at least two decades; change happens overnight.

I often say that history wasn't made by women who played it safe. There are several reasons why professional women may become less essential in their field:

- Resistance to change and lack of adaptability, which we've addressed
- Failure to innovate and update skills
- Lack of continuous learning

Fostering a growth mindset involves viewing challenges as opportunities for learning and growth. Embrace feedback, learn from your mistakes, and seek self-improvement. Here are some strategies to help you remain essential:

Stay updated: Stay informed about industry trends, advancements, and changes. Subscribe to relevant newsletters, follow industry thought leaders, and attend conferences or webinars to stay abreast of the latest developments. Carve out fifteen minutes of each workday to stay up to date.

Adopt technology: Technology is constantly evolving and transforming industries. Embrace new tools, software, and digital platforms that can enhance your productivity and effectiveness. Stay open to learning modern technologies that can streamline your work processes.

Continuous learning: Commit to lifelong learning and professional development. Acquire new skills, certifications, or qualifications relevant to your field. Your *Now, Near, Next Blueprint* should include these goals and commitments.

 Actualize Potential:

Where do you need to focus additional time or investment to bolster your relevance?

Remember, remaining essential in your profession is an ongoing process. You can position yourself as an indispensable professional by consistently developing your skills, staying adaptable, and providing value.

Conclusion

A plan that actualizes your full potential comes with risks and rewards. The more intentionally you prepare for your *Now, Near, Next*, the more control you gain over the pace and course of your journey. Getting comfortable with change, having the courage to make bold moves, and embracing a growth mindset will enable you to adapt, innovate, and stay relevant.

As we move to chapter nine, we will address the reality that life happens and is not always as planned, the importance of self-care throughout your *Now, Near, Next,* and taking time to celebrate your progress to date and the continued actualization of your potential moving forward.

Reflection: Take Risks

I began to understand that taking risks is part of success even if you occasionally fail.

— **Jona Van Deun,** Managing Partner, Prairie Coast Strategies, LLC

Jona Van Deun, managing partner of Prairie Coast Strategies, LLC, advises clients on grassroots, government and public affairs, and special projects nationwide.

With an extensive background across public affairs and nonprofits, Jona has previously held leadership positions with the U.S. Chamber of Commerce, the White House, and Capitol Hill and was most recently the president of the Nebraska Tech Collaborative (NTC) within the Aksarben Foundation.

Throughout her thirty-year career, Jona has supplied strategic expertise and advice to various trade associations and Fortune 500 companies, including 3M Company, the Pillsbury Company, DCI Group, and the Property Casualty Insurers Association (PCI). Jona also served as Director of Coalitions for Koch Companies Public Sector.

As a graduate and member of the Board of Trustees of the College of St. Benedict in Minnesota, one of the few remaining women's liberal arts colleges in the U.S., Jona focuses her charitable and volunteer activities toward programs that attract and develop women for leadership positions in government and business.

When I was selected to lead the Nebraska Tech Collaborative, which is focused on enriching the state's economic position through selecting and retaining tech talent, I thought I'd finally made it! The business leaders chose me and trusted me with their vision and money. This is what I worked for my entire career—president.

However, I had doubts. I was afraid of the consequences if I failed. This was a high-stakes, visible role on the statewide political stage. I was also emotionally invested. I wanted our work to be meaningful, impactful, and rewarding for Nebraska. I wanted the outside world to see our efforts as significant.

Pushing the fear aside, I stepped forward. Charged with leading this organization, I was ready to actualize the concepts that had been discussed for years. Within three years, a vibrant technology ecosystem materialized with a statewide impact. Success.

However, after three years of working at breakneck speed and helping to realize the vision, I began questioning my long-term fit. My strength and excitement come from building and innovating, not maintaining. Yet the organization was moving into a steady state.

I shifted my attention to other opportunities for meaningful change, but there wasn't an appetite for the kind of transformation that I wanted to lead. I felt defeated. And I was terrified of being labeled as a failure.

Over several months, the feeling of failure was palpable. I began worrying about demonstrating success. My ideas as a leader seemed less and less relevant to the organization. I wasn't happy. I couldn't see a way forward. I kept thinking that good leaders don't leave their jobs. Good leadership is navigating through challenges. Would I be seen as a quitter? Would my contemporaries say I couldn't handle it?

After some reflection, I realized that good leadership means recognizing when it is time to move on. It was OK to graduate from one opportunity and pursue another. The talents that had led to my early successes would be highly valuable in my *Next*.

However, the fear of failure I had harbored had another repercussion—exhaustion. It all had caught up with me—hard. So, I took a risk and quit, taking two months off to rest and reflect.

As I thought through my experience, I began to understand that taking risks is part of growth, and failure is a matter of perspective. That fear was the push I needed to take stock of my career and life and lead me to my *Next*. Today, I am excited (and apprehensive) about starting my own company, thrilled at the prospect of trying several new things, and excited to return to government and grassroots work.

If you are willing to make bold choices and take risks, you are guaranteed to experience fear and discomfort at some point. You may even experience a feeling of failure. Although I like to consider Henry Ford's perspective, "Failure is simply the opportunity to begin again, this time more intelligently."

Take risks, learn from the experience, recharge, adapt, and drive on.

CHAPTER NINE

Bolster Resilience and Agility

A woman is like a tea bag; you never know how strong it is until it's in hot water.

— **Eleanor Roosevelt,** former First Lady of the United States, diplomat, and activist

CHAPTER NINE OFFERS A REALITY CHECK for the skeptics and those who have been blown off course because life is messy. As we have journeyed together up to this point, the lessons have been forward-focused, aspirational, and planful. It is at this juncture that we address the derailers of life and provide practical insight on how to get back on the path.

Among the women we spoke to, several experienced significant career disrupters. Some left the workforce or went part-time after starting a family; others moved across the country or outside the U.S. to support their spouses' jobs. Some of these life events were planned, and others were unexpected.

Having a plan is an essential step in actualizing your *Next.* At the same time, exercising resilience and remaining open to alternative paths, taking care of yourself, and celebrating the little wins are critical to fully realizing your potential.

For some, this chapter will be reflective; for others, it may be just in time, and for some, it will be just in case. However, at the risk of being doom-and-gloom, the reality is that each one of us will be blown off course at some point on our journey. Preparing for disruption is another essential step in professional intentionality.

Develop a Base-Camp Outlook

A few years ago, at a strategic planning meeting, I was introduced to the concept of developing a base-camp mindset. The metaphor is that you have charted a path to the summit; however, throughout your journey, you stop at base-camps to rest, reenergize, and assess the environment—often intentionally, and other times because you are forced to. Depending on the conditions, you may reroute or consider alternative approaches to the summit. Depending on the headwinds or opportunities in front of you, you may change your destination entirely.

Reflecting on many of the stories shared by the women we interviewed, life events often changed the trajectories of their paths. And just as there are many routes to reaching the summit, you can realize your *Next* via many paths.

NEXT

Milestone Six Basecamp
Milestone Five Basecamp
Milestone Four Basecamp
Milestone Three Basecamp
Milestone Two Basecamp
Milestone One Basecamp

A base-camp mindset acknowledges that progress may not always be linear. It embraces the idea of iterating and adapting along the way. Instead of rigidly sticking to the original plan, be open to looking up and adjusting based on added information, feedback, or changing circumstances.

Use your *Now, Near, Next Blueprint* as your metaphorical map. Consider each milestone as a base-camp opportunity. During each of these intentional "stops," take a moment to reflect and consider these important actions:

Assess Progress: Evaluate the effectiveness of your strategies and tactics. Assess whether you're on track, identify areas for improvement, and consider adjustments or course corrections as needed. Embrace the concept "fail fast, learn quickly" to refine your approach. Jona's reflection provides an excellent example of stopping to reevaluate the situation, appreciating that the current path was no longer appropriate, and charting a new course.

Seek Feedback and Input: Seek feedback and input from your supporters. Engage in open and transparent communication to gather insights, alternative perspectives, and suggestions for improvement. Mentors and coaches can help you check in with yourself to assess if the road you are on is still the right direction.

Years ago, I was having an investment conversation with a woman on my human resources team. In seeking to understand her true passion, I learned that she wanted to be an esthetician. Together, we devised a plan that provided her the flexibility to attend courses while continuing to perform in her day job until she was licensed. Years later, she sent me a note thanking me for providing her the feedback, flexibility, and push to do what she truly loves.

Celebrate Achievements: Celebrate your achievements and milestones along the way. Recognize and acknowledge the progress you've made both individually and collectively. Taking time to celebrate can be the fuel you need to continue your journey. We will cover this in more detail later in this chapter.

Remember, a base-camp mindset embraces flexibility, adaptability, and learning throughout the journey toward your *Next*. By breaking down your plan, seeking feedback, and regularly evaluating progress, you can remain agile and adjust your approach as necessary. Depending on your assessment of your current path during a base-camp stop, you may elect to reroute.

Navigate Rerouting

There is some magic and lessons learned in every challenge, hardship, and everything that doesn't go as you think it should. When you reflect on it, think, how is this happening for me, not to me.

— **Kara Bunde-Dunn**, CEO, karmic leader

So here is a plot twist that neither you, the reader, nor I saw coming at this point. In a very strange turn of fate, as we were within weeks of sending this manuscript to our editor, my corporate executive position was eliminated. The position that I have referred to throughout the first eight chapters, the role that I had been balancing and prioritizing ahead of writing this book.

I was initially in shock. I experienced every one of the grief stages over and over again for the better part of a week. However, if I am being honest, my preparedness for my *Next* was in large part to ensure that I had a plan if I found myself a casualty of the organizational changes. The possibility that my role, talent, and experience may no longer be a fit under new leadership was not lost on me.

I know how often new leaders make changes in structure and among their executive teams. Surrounding themselves with individuals that complement their aces and spaces, and that of the teams', is critical in a transition of leadership. In many ways, I had been feeling much like what Jona expressed in her chapter eight reflection. I had graduated. The timing, however, was unexpected. I had been blown off course.

This was not the plan. How was I going to pivot? Where would I start? Talk about a reality check and the immediate requirement for me to "drink my own champagne."

As I picked up this manuscript seeking wisdom and solace, it became clear that I had fundamental work to do—beginning with Maslow's Hierarchy of Needs.

Working through the emotional impact of a situation that disrupts your path is job number one. I spent the better part of the first week in a daze. Frankly, the whole situation was surreal and disorienting. My path forward seemed cloudy at first, and I immediately went into survival mode.

Beginning with a list of expenses that I could do without or scale back, I began to cancel memberships and change the frequency of discretionary purchases. With an uncertain future,

I knew I would need to sell my home and find something more affordable. I scheduled an appointment with a financial planner to review my retirement plans and determine whether I could afford to transition to my *Next* now or needed to find a new corporate position for a few more years. All of these actions gave me back my agency and power over that which I could control.

As I began to work through the physiological and safety concerns, I began grieving the loss of the daily connection with my team. My sense of belonging and community felt severed. I had worked with many leaders and most of my team for over a decade. However, the relationships I had built and invested in over the years were strong. I was encouraged and inspired by literally hundreds of text messages, emails, cards, and phone calls from people inside and outside of the organization.

As I reread chapter five, I found motivation to connect with my network more intentionally, life's board of directors, coaches and mentors. These connections offered wisdom, advice, support, and praise when I most needed it. They also have been a great source of referrals and references.

Even with the support of my community, self-doubt crept in like a bad dream. Change that throws you off course can come with some emotional baggage that you need to unpack, challenging your self-esteem. Referring back to chapter seven, I spent a lot of time pausing, protesting, pivoting, and praying. I'm quite sure crying was in there too.

To energize forward momentum, I forced myself to resume a daily routine of getting up early, showering, having a list of purposeful activities, writing, and rereading chapters two through nine. Standing at a new base-camp, chapter by chapter, I considered which summit to pursue and then renewed or revised my goals accordingly. Let's just say that I've spent some additional time in prayerful reflection on the following:

Reflect on Your Values and Goals: Take the time to clarify your values, long-term aspirations, and core goals. Understand what truly matters to you in your career and life. Trust your gut and listen to your intuition. This self-awareness will help you make informed decisions regarding rerouting your career path.

I found myself entertaining opportunities that would have been the path of least resistance but, deep down, didn't excite me. I had to determine if, at this point in my life, I was prepared to start a new corporate position and put off my *Next* or make some significant lifestyle changes and accelerate my timeline (see chapter two).

Embrace Transferable Skills: Identify the skills and experiences you have acquired throughout your career that are transferable to different industries or roles. Highlight these skills and emphasize their relevance in new contexts. This will enable you to pivot more quickly if you change directions (see chapter three).

This step was an important awakening. It is easy to limit yourself by considering only your current or most recent role, but broadening your perspective of your complete collection of skills and knowledge can open a host of possibilities. Fortunately, because I was working on my *Now*, I had made progress preparing myself for my *Next*.

Revise your *Now, Near, Next Blueprint*: If the life event has completely changed your *Next*, it is time to review chapters two through four and begin again. Taking this step, although potentially challenging, is important to continued forward progress. If the event has accelerated the path to your *Next*, take time to revise your timeline and prioritize your action steps.

After prayerful consideration, I made the decision to fully pursue my *Next* now, putting positive energy toward organizational and leadership consulting. As part of my discernment process, I updated my *Now, Near, Next Blueprint.* You will notice a couple of things. First, I reorganized my action items. Some things will be more important immediately. I also moved some of the more ambitious action steps to what may become my next *Next*.

My ability to consolidate a three-year plan into a nine-month plan was made possible by two critical factors:

1. My time was now fully dedicated to launching my *Next*.
2. I had made significant progress in actualizing my *Now*, giving me a tremendous head start.

	9-Month Plan ~~3-Year Plan~~	Action
NOW	First Six Months ~~Jan., Year One–Dec., Year Two~~	✓ Establish an LLC ✓ Obtain Board Certified Coaching (BCC) credential ✓ Develop initial website ✓ Write first book ✓ Engage in financial planning • Engage supporters • Develop a business and marketing plan • Broaden network • Attend Impact Eleven
NEAR	Three Months ~~Jan.–Dec., Year Three~~	• Book launch • Engage public speaking • Advance website design • Strengthen financial plan
NEXT	Ongoing to new *Next*	• Begin second book • Develop podcast • Seek public board opportunity

Stay Agile and Open to Opportunities: Be open to new opportunities that may arise unexpectedly. Keep your eye on the job market, industry trends, and emerging fields. Actively seek opportunities to take on new projects, assignments, or responsibilities that can broaden your skill set and open doors to alternative career paths (chapters four–eight).

The truth: curveballs will come, and mine hit me square in the eyes when I wasn't looking. However, they can offer the wake-up call that pulls you forward into a more fulfilling direction if you use the event to your advantage, or so I'm learning and embracing.

My conviction to help women energize self-agency, ignite intentionality, and actualize potential has never been stronger. Had I not begun planning for my *Next*, I would have had only one path: to hurry up and find a new corporate job, which I determined was the last thing I wanted to do. Instead, I found myself at an unexpected base-camp, charting a new path, and picking up the pace. The summit remains in view, I have a plan, and the future is bright.

Remember, your *Now, Near, Next Blueprint* establishes your desired outcome and helps you prepare, but being flexible and open to new possibilities can lead to unexpected opportunities and personal growth. By embracing change, seeking continuous learning, and maintaining a proactive mindset even when faced with adversity, you can navigate career rerouting with confidence and adaptability.

Exercise Holistic Self-Care

Just enjoy your life, laugh, be silly, and don't take things or yourself so seriously.

—Ann Elizabeth Mohart, MD

We have covered much territory up to this point in the book. You've been challenged to let go of guilt, carve out time for yourself, identify and invest in your natural talents, develop a plan for your *Next*, seek supporters, show up confidently, and take risks. With all that we take on, it is not surprising that a 2020 Women in the Workplace study revealed that women feel consistently more exhausted and burnt out at work than their male counterparts. So if you feel overwhelmed, remember that this framework is intended to meet you where you are and go at your pace.

What is most critical is healthy forward motion. Being the best version of yourself is impossible if you are completely worn out. Given the pressure of balancing work and home life, women must prioritize self-care as a nonnegotiable part of their day. Part of maintaining momentum toward your *Next* is holistic self-care. And while this book was not written as self-help, we would be remiss if we did not, at minimum, bring attention to the most important dimensions of wellness.

Employ a Wheel of Well-Being

You can't pour from an empty cup.

— Unknown

The Wheel of Wellness, or the Dimensions of Wellness, is a concept developed and expanded upon by various individuals and organizations. Early credit is attributed to Dr. Bill Hettler, cofounder of the National Wellness Institute (NWI), who introduced the Dimensions of Wellness in the 1970s. Thirty years later, psychologists Jane Myers, Thomas Sweeney, and Melvin Witmer (2000) broadened the concept to focus on overall lifestyle choices. Several versions of the Wheel of Wellness are available and have been modified by consultancies and institutions.

Wellness and well-being are two related concepts that focus on a person's overall health and quality of life. While they are often used interchangeably, from our perspective, they have slightly different meanings and implications.

Wellness refers to the active pursuit of health. Wellness emphasizes self-care practices and proactive steps to maintain and improve health and vitality. On the other hand, well-being refers to the overall state of being happy, healthy, and prosperous. It is a broader concept encompassing various dimensions of a person's life. Individual experiences, life satisfaction, purpose, positive emotions, and a supportive social network influence well-being. It is a state of optimal functioning and fulfillment in different areas of life.

Spiritual Well-Being: Spiritual well-being is about finding meaning and purpose in life. Spiritual health is a deeply personal aspect of well-being, and it can be nurtured through various practices and beliefs depending on an individual's values and cultural background. Different people may find spiritual fulfillment through religious practices, meditation, nature, artistic expression, or other means. The key is cultivating a sense of connection, purpose, and inner peace that resonates with one's beliefs and values.

Emotional Well-Being: Emotional well-being focuses on effectively understanding and managing emotions. It involves the awareness and healthy expression of feelings, developing resilience, and maintaining positive relationships. Incorporating mindfulness techniques like meditation, deep-breathing exercises, or yoga into your daily routine can help reduce stress, increase focus, and promote overall well-being.

In addition, take regular breaks from technology and create designated tech-free zones or hours in your day. Health experts suggest that limiting screen time can help reduce stress, improve sleep quality, and foster a more significant presence in your daily life.

According to the National Sleep Foundation, try eliminating technology one hour before bed. The blue light emitted by electronic devices such as smartphones, tablets, and computers can suppress the production of melatonin, a hormone that regulates sleep-wake cycles. Exposure to blue light before bed can disrupt the body's natural circadian rhythm and make it harder to fall asleep. Not to mention that engaging in screen-related activities such as scrolling through social media, watching videos, or playing stimulating games can be mentally and emotionally engaging, leading to poor sleep quality and difficulties falling asleep.

Most important, if you are feeling overwhelmed, anxious, or depressed, seek help from a friend, therapist, counselor, or clergy, or dial the 988 crisis lifeline. The stigma associated with mental health concerns is literally killing us. We must recognize that our mental health is just as important, real, and valid as our physical health.

Intellectual Well-Being: Intellectual well-being involves lifelong learning, critical thinking, and expanding knowledge and skills. It encompasses intellectual curiosity, creativity, and problem-solving abilities. You activate your intellectual health by looking up and forward and putting your *Now, Near, Next Blueprint* into action.

Physical Well-Being: This dimension relates to the physical aspects of health and the body's overall functioning. I don't know about you, but I have two "tells" when I am overwhelmed, overworked, and not taking enough time for self-care. First, I get a terrible canker sore on my lip. Or I wake up with incredible jaw, ear, or tooth pain from grinding my teeth. Neither is pleasant.

Take care of your body by exercising regularly, eating nutritious meals, getting enough sleep, moving, and staying hydrated. Invest time in finding a primary care physician you connect with and get an annual physical. Prioritize preventive health checkups and listen to your body's needs. As a breast cancer survivor, I can attest that early detection saves lives. You can't be good for anyone else if you are not healthy.

Social Well-Being: Social well-being refers to having a supportive and satisfying social network. It involves developing and maintaining healthy relationships, effective communication, and a sense of belonging in various social groups.

In 2023, the U.S. Surgeon General declared loneliness and isolation an epidemic. Dr. Murthy's report cites numerous physical health consequences associated with poor social support, including a 29 percent increase in risk of heart disease, a 32 percent increase in risk of stroke, and a 50 percent increase in risk of developing dementia for older adults.

Leaning into your social network, including your life's board of directors, is critical. Showing up and seeking opportunities for in-person connections are also vital. Unwinding the isolation habits formed during the pandemic is essential to social well-being.

Financial Well-Being: Women often face career interruptions due to caregiving responsibilities such as raising children or caring for elderly parents. These interruptions can affect their income, retirement savings, and long-term financial planning. Additionally, life events like a job elimination, divorce, or widowhood may necessitate adjustments to financial plans. Financial well-being is effectively managing one's financial resources and achieving financial stability. It involves budgeting, saving, and making informed income, expenses, and investment decisions.

If at all possible, maintaining a financial safety net, such as an emergency fund or savings, can give you a sense of security and flexibility when making career transitions or pursuing new ventures. Financial stability can alleviate some concerns associated with taking risks or deviating from your initial career plan.

Consider working with a financial planner or advisor who specializes in helping women with their financial goals. These resources don't have to be expensive. Some company employee assistance programs (EAPs), banks, churches, and retirement plan administrators offer support or courses on financial planning. A professional can provide personalized advice, help create a comprehensive financial plan, and guide investment strategies and risk management.

Whether you are living comfortably within or outside of your means or struggling to keep up, financial planning is a critical. So abandon pride or shame at the door. Don't leave your agency to others, especially when the unexpected changes the rules.

Wheel of Well-Being in Action

A woman's health is her capital.

— **Harriet Beecher Stowe,** American author and abolitionist

In keeping with the broader definition, we introduce the Wheel of Well-Being. Regardless of the version used, the benefits of holistic self-care are in its practical application. Taking time in your daily reflection to check in on the six dimensions of well-being will reinforce areas of gratitude and isolate places that require focused attention.

In addition to your daily reflection, consider completing an evaluation of your well-being in each of the dimensions on a quarterly basis. Assess your satisfaction with and the priority of each dimension. Note that physical and emotional well-being must be rated a minimum of a "3" priority. It is never OK to sacrifice your emotional or physical well-being. If for any reason your physical or emotional well-being does not feel like a priority, seek input from your primary care physician and a licensed professional.

Determine the area of greatest opportunity among the seven dimensions and commit to just one small investment you will make in yourself for the next ninety days. For example, if you are disappointed in your exercise routine, establish a goal to take the stairs instead of the elevator for the next three months or complete a seven-minute exercise routine three days a week. If you are feeling out of touch socially, commit to booking a lunch or happy hour once a month throughout the quarter. Whatever you commit to should be fulfilling and life-giving, not another burden to add to your plate.

Dimensions	Satisfaction 1 = Low 5= High	Priority 1 = Low 5 = High	Action 90-Day Commitment
Spiritual			
Emotional		3, 4, 5	
Intellectual			
Physical		3, 4, 5	
Social			
Financial			

PLOT THE DIMENSIONS BASED ON YOUR RATINGS

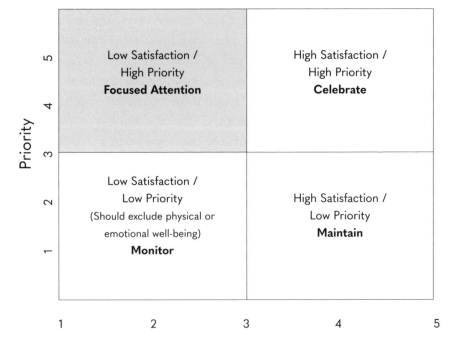

Actualize Potential:

Where do you need to invest additional time in your well-being over the next ninety days?

Remember, self-care is a personal journey, and what works for one person may not work for another. Experiment with different practices and find a holistic self-care routine that resonates with you and supports your well-being as a professional woman. Self-care is not an all-or-nothing practice. According to the National Institute of Mental Health, even small acts of self-care can have a cumulative positive effect on reducing stress, lowering risk of illness, and increasing overall energy. By prioritizing self-care

> These dimensions are interconnected and influence one another. Achieving a balance across all dimensions is considered essential for overall well-being. The Well-being Wheel serves as a tool to assess and identify areas for improvement in these various dimensions, guiding you toward a more holistic approach to self-care.

and involving others in supporting your needs, you can overcome the tendency to neglect self-care and create a healthier and more balanced lifestyle.

Celebrate Success

In leadership development, I often remind participants that "behavior that gets noticed gets repeated." That same principle can be applied to ourselves. When we achieve a goal or experience success, including small victories, we activate the brain's reward system and promote dopamine release. This can enhance our feelings of accomplishment, satisfaction, and happiness. Dopamine in the brain can also contribute to increased focus, attention, and engagement in the task at hand, further supporting ongoing efforts and progress.

By recognizing and celebrating our progress even in small increments, we stay engaged and motivated to continue working toward our goals. As we celebrate our achievements, we build confidence in our capabilities and develop a belief that we can consistently engage in the desired behavior. This increased self-efficacy supports habit formation by fostering a positive mindset and reducing self-doubt.

S.P.I.C.E.

For the acknowledgment of small victories to have an impact, you must be intentional. Try using the S.P.I.C.E. model when patting yourself or others on the back.

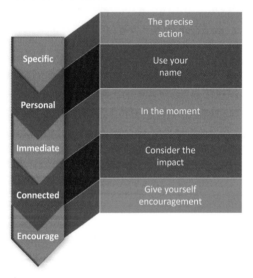

[Your name], you did it. You just finished reading chapter eight and documented your commitments on the Now, Near, Next Blueprint. You are following through on investing unapologetic,

guilt-free time in yourself. As a result, you realize your full potential, becoming the best version of yourself for those who love and count on you. Keep up the great progress. You've got this!

It's important to note that while celebrating small wins can support habit formation, consistency and repetition are still essential for habit development. Regularly engaging in the desired behavior and acknowledging and celebrating progress will help solidify the habit. To celebrate personal and professional success, consider the following strategies:

Acknowledge your achievements: Take time to reflect on your accomplishments and credit yourself for your progress. Recognize the milestones you've reached and the goals you've accomplished. I like to track things in percentage completion or other measures showing progress toward a larger purpose. With authoring this book, I tracked progress based on each chapter completed. You can record these on your *Now, Near, Next Blueprint* or in a daily journal.

> "People think that you have to do something huge, like go to Africa and build a school, but you can make a small change in a day. If you change Wednesday, then you change Thursday. Pretty soon it's a week, then a month, then a year. It's bite-size, as opposed to feeling like you have to turn your life inside out to make changes."
>
> —Hoda Kotb is an American broadcast journalist and television personality

Share your success: Share your achievements with others who have supported and cheered you on. Celebrate with friends, family, or colleagues who have been part of your journey and can share in your joy. My mom, sister, and adult children are on a regular text update regarding my writing milestones.

Treat yourself: Reward yourself for your success. It could be something small like indulging in your favorite meal, pampering yourself with a spa day, or buying something you've wanted. I recall that following a promotion many years ago, I got my nails done for the first time. I remember the smile it put on my leader's face to see how much that self-indulgent treat meant to me. Choose a reward that aligns with your personal preferences and values.

Reflect and set new goals: Use the celebration to reflect on your journey and set new goals. Refer to your *Now, Near, Next Blueprint.* Consider what you've learned, what you want to achieve next, and how you can continue to grow personally and professionally. We are already envisioning our next book, focused on women approaching the end of their career.

 Actualize Potential:

What is one small win you will celebrate today?

Remember, celebrating success is not about bragging or comparing yourself to others. It's about acknowledging your progress, embracing the joy of achievement, and using it as fuel to keep pushing forward. Why wait? This is a perfect time to celebrate! You have nearly concluded a book that is 100 percent focused on investing in *you.* Congratulations!

Conclusion

Big, deep breath. We have covered much ground. And while I am an optimist by nature, I'm also a realist. So in this closing chapter, we have offered a reality check. All the best planning in the world is subject to life's unexpected twists and turns, as my most recent turn of events would demonstrate. Preparing for regular check-ins, course corrections, and rerouting will be necessary. Life is also messy. Taking time to reflect on the six dimensions of well-being is vital to being the best version of yourself and fully actualizing your potential.

Finally, there is so much to celebrate. Don't wait for monumental acts of heroics. Take time to celebrate the little wins of actualizing your potential. As you conclude, take a moment to relish in the passionate, talented, brilliant woman you are today and reflect on the incredible version you will be in your *Next*.

Reflection: Bolster Resilience

Love yourself for who you are today and who you will become.

— Ann Elizabeth Mohart, MD

Dr. Ann Elizabeth Mohart is an emergency medicine physician who has worked for Mercy for twenty years. For the past three years, she has served as chief medical officer for Mercy Hospital in Washington, Missouri.

Ann Elizabeth is married to John Mohart, MD, and they have four children, ages four to fifteen. She loves spending time on their family farm and gardening when not at work.

I recently spotted a book on a shelf entitled *Letters to My Younger Self*. It got me thinking about what advice I would give the younger version of myself from where I stand today: all the lessons learned, the life lived, the mistakes, the thrills, and the misadventures. In reflection, I am a completely different woman today than I was twenty years ago. Which, I suppose, is the point. I am wiser and more empathic and have learned what matters to me and what I stand for.

Letting go of my younger self and growing into the woman I am today was sometimes painful and felt like a loss—it felt messy. But the parts of me left behind were necessary for growth. What I gained in return was far more valuable and far more lasting.

I believe all women go through this metamorphosis. For some, transformation is an organic process of growth over time. For others, life events thrust you forward. Either way, navigating through the transition is a process of surrendering—letting go. So letting go and embracing grace is where all the wisdom and beauty lie. What have I let go of that I clung to as the younger version of myself? And what would I tell her?

While I am still learning and changing, from where I stand today in the middle spot of life, I would tell my younger self the following:

Ann Elizabeth, most battles and struggles you will wage will exist within your mind. Be incredibly careful about that terrain. Women can be so hard on themselves—holding themselves to unattainable ideals that they are fed from birth. The sooner you can release the idea that your value and worth are determined by surface details, the more joy you will have. As you move through your thirties and forties, you will be much more loving toward your body. It matters to feel good and be healthy, so that should be a priority, but the drive to get there should be about self-love—not hustling for worth.

Figure out who you are and what matters to you and never abandon those standards to be accepted or fit in. You will be better off alone in the wilderness than exchanging your deepest identity and values for a false belonging. The sooner you can achieve that and be unapologetic about who you are, the fiercer you will be. Over time, you will shred your fears about what others think. That will be less and less of a motivator. Bravely hold what you believe in, and when you arrive there—knowing who you are—external validation will no longer be required. It becomes irrelevant.

Have fun. Laugh. Period. Don't take yourself or life so seriously. You are a perfectionist; use that to your advantage but recognize how little control you have over the trajectory of your life. Allow spontaneous moments of bliss instead of trying to stay on the course of what you believe your story should be. Embracing grace is about moving with the current of life and letting it take you to unexpected places. Trusting the flow of the universe is highly recommended. No one is ever fully in control, and the sooner you accept that, the easier life gets.

People matter. The most important decision you will ever make will be who you allow to come into your life. Surround yourself with people that feel good. Use your heart and gut here more than your brain. Do not overthink this—just trust how a person makes you feel. If they feel good, get them in your life as much as possible. If you feel bad when you are with them, that is where boundaries come in. Get good at setting limits and building boundaries regarding toxic people. You should use the word "no" like a machete. Build your community and belong there.

Lastly, there is no glory in staying locked in your comfort zone. Your comfort zone can become a prison. Life is meant to be lived, but when one really risks that, it can feel like pain, failure, or rejection. Those are signs that you are growing and challenging yourself. The road to success and growth is paved with failures. Do not misinterpret that experience as a reflection of inadequacies. This is you growing. You grow through the pain. The pain can sometimes be where all the magic happens. Lean into it and move through it to the other side. And once you are through the other side, you will be a different woman, a better, wiser, older version of your magnificent self. And all along the way, never forget that you are worthy.

Love yourself for who you are today and who you will become. At the end of the day—as women—that should be the lifelong message we have for ourselves and one another.

Section Three: Next—Actualize Potential

Take a moment to consider all the ways we have of bolstering resilience in section three. Pause to revisit the personal reflections. Using the *Now, Near, Next* Companion Guide, or a journal, check to ensure you have documented all the quick action steps and created accountability for yourself. In addition, it is time to live into your *Now, Near, Next.* Your *Blueprint* provides a road map; print it, keep it handy, and review and refine it regularly. You choose your pace; just make sure that you continue your forward momentum when you reach the last page.

 Personal Reflection

 Take Quick Action

 Chart in *Now, Near, Next Blueprint*

Chapter Seven:

🌩 Where do you need to place additional focus to develop self-efficacy further?

🌩 What affirming statement can you incorporate into your self-talk, using your first name, to promote positivity and momentum in your life?

🌩 In what ways do you need to show up more intentionally?

👠 What is a common word or phrase that you need to remove from your communication style?

Chapter Eight:

👠 What is your greatest fear related to your *Next*? What is one thing you will do to harness that energy and mitigate that fear?

👠 How prepared are you to respond to a job solicitation or actively pursue an opportunity of interest? What will you do now to increase your readiness?

🌩 Where will you focus additional time or investment to bolster your relevance?

Chapter Nine:

👠 Where do you need to invest additional time in your well-being for the next ninety days?

👠 What is one small win you will celebrate today?

CONCLUSION

Doing the best at this moment puts you in the best place for the next moment.

— **Oprah Winfrey,** American talk show host, producer, actress, and author

IT LOOKS LIKE WE'VE MADE IT! We have identified the steps to reaching our *Next* one page at a time, keeping in mind energizing self-agency, igniting intentionality, and actualizing potential, which is a work in progress. Like kinetic energy, the positive force that moves you into motion propels you forward. The goal is to continue advancing and maintain momentum.

As I reflect on the lessons learned over the past nine chapters, I'm reminded of how much intentionality it takes to unwind longtime habits and conditioning. It is one thing to document well-researched tools and challenge new behavior; it is another to drink your own champagne. Here are my personal reflections.

Chapter one encourages making peace with choices, establishing boundaries, and asking for and receiving help. While I have made some strides in this area, I'm working on not overcommitting out of guilt or obligation and more openly embracing grace.

Chapter two requires getting clear on your mission, vision, and values. Taking the time to write down and proclaim my purpose was liberating. I was reminded of what is most important to me. Being committed to my *why* now is a compass to ensure I'm on the right path as I determine whether I accelerate my *Next* or have an intermediate step in between.

Perhaps the greatest learning in **chapter three** was related to professional brand. I have long understood the importance of living into natural talent and presenting oneself authentically. What was further revealed to me in the writing and research was how your brand is influenced by actions. When you don't set boundaries, you create a persona that others come to expect. And not everyone is going to like you—be at peace with that.

Chapter four gave us the tools and template to chart our journey. At this point, I had to reconcile the desire to share with the world that I was writing a book and the feeling that it would appear boastful or self-promoting. Not surprisingly, the news was met with pride and joy from loved ones and a few snarky comments and envy from others. I was reminded that other people's opinions of me are none of my business.

With the reminder in **chapter five** of how important supporters are in each of our lives, I've made a commitment to strengthen my network. Taking time to more intentionally foster relationships is a priority. I've been so busy working that I've failed to invest in my community. I'm planning an actual meeting among the women on my life's board of directors. If nothing else, can you imagine the incredible memories and laughter that will be shared over bottles of exceptional wine?

A significant lesson and reflection for me in **chapter six** was the concept of volume versus value. Because of my tendency to get bored if I'm not learning, I have historically taken on projects or assignments that added work without intrinsic benefit. As

I continue to recalibrate my *Now, Near, Next,* I must regularly determine how much I can and should take on.

In reflection, **chapter seven** was where I needed to spend some real dedicated time. Dealing with the ending of my corporate career and having the confidence to potentially venture out on my own took intentional focus. The concepts of positive self-talk and efficacy were powerful reminders.

Embarking on authoring a book felt like the type of bold move encouraged in **chapter eight**. Kimberly and I have invested time, talent, and treasure into this labor of love. The financial commitment, endless hours of writing, and careful balance of personal and professional responsibilities required agility and faith.

If one woman finds the inspiration to actualize her potential, this will have been a risk worth taking, and one that I'm prepared to continue. And while I may not have taken Barbara Walters's chair all those years ago, I now have my sights set on sitting across from Gayle King with Kimberly, sharing our delight in being chosen as one of Oprah's book club picks. Like my daughter, "I have no small dreams!"

Chapter nine reminds us that life is messy, and all of the best-laid plans can be disrupted. My conviction to encourage women to have a thoughtful plan was exponentially reinforced. Having looked up and forward with a focus on my *Next* provided an alternative path when the circumstances changed.

Furthermore, we must take holistic care of ourselves and celebrate. When writing this chapter, an essential reminder was the importance of small wins. Each chapter represented a milestone and an opportunity to acknowledge progress. With the full manuscript going to the editor, pampering and celebration are on the horizon. Who knows? Maybe Kimberly and I will return to the sandy beaches of Mexico and begin our next *Next.*

Where are you on this journey? What are your reflections?

How will you apply what you have learned? How are you feeling? If you are energized, great! If you are overwhelmed, we've got you.

As you tackle your *Now, Near, Next,* break it down into manageable goals. Keep in mind, this book is segmented by each phase: Section One—Now, Section Two—Near, and Section Three—Next. Your *Blueprint* will help ensure you aren't trying to take on the learning from all nine chapters simultaneously.

Suffice it to say that among our contributors' nine hundred years of combined experience as successful women authors, professionals, entrepreneurs, and educators, we are all continually learning and growing. It takes time and effort to dispel or disarm societal, self-induced, and habitual limitations. Have patience with yourself but persistence with your progress. Let's go:

- Review your *Now, Near, Next* Companion Guide or notes.
- Complete your *Now, Near, Next Blueprint.*
- Keep it handy to share, monitor, and modify it as you gain momentum.
- Remember, go at your pace based on your current circumstances and make intentional stops at base-camps.
- Empower other women by boldly telling your story as you energize self-agency, ignite intentionality, and actualize your potential.
- Buckle up for an exciting new ride.

You've got this. Take a moment to celebrate this focus on you. *Cheers* to what is *Next!*

Do not follow where the path may lead. Go instead where there is no path and leave a trail.

— **Ralph Waldo Emerson,** American philosopher

AFTERWORD

By Kimberly K. Rath, MBA, Coauthor

Over thirty-two years ago, I heard a profound statement from my four-year-old daughter, Makenzie Rath, as I stood washing dishes with my back turned to her. She said, "Listen with your eyes," a message that still resonates today. It holds a deeper meaning that goes beyond its literal interpretation. It reminds us to be fully present, engaged, and attentive in our interactions, not just with others but also with ourselves and our aspirations.

As mid-career women, we often find ourselves at a crossroads, caught between the demands of our current roles and the desire to explore new possibilities. In this phase, it becomes crucial to listen with our eyes, not only to what is being said externally but also to the whispers of our own dreams and aspirations. Listening with our eyes means being attuned to the subtle cues and opportunities that present themselves in our professional journeys. It means looking beyond the limitations imposed by self-doubt and fear and instead opening our minds to the vast array of possibilities that lie ahead. It means embracing a growth mindset in which we believe in our capacity to learn, adapt, and succeed.

Mid-career is a pivotal time to reevaluate our goals, values, and passions. By listening with our eyes, we can identify areas of growth, potential career paths, and opportunities for personal and professional development. It allows us to tap into our intuition and explore new avenues that align with our talents and values. Moreover, listening with our eyes empowers us to be present in the moment. It encourages us to be fully engaged in our work, relationships, and personal growth. Being present allows us to cultivate deeper connections, seize opportunities, and make informed decisions about our futures.

I feel honored and delighted to embark on the *Now, Near, Next* journey alongside Cynthia Bentzen-Mercer. Together, we have crafted a blueprint designed to illuminate the path for women, enabling them to amplify their potentiality with intentional positive energy. Throughout this journey, we have shared laughter and tears as we listened to remarkable stories from women—stories filled with challenges, appreciation, and inspiration.

So as mid-career women, let us remember the wisdom in Makenzie's words, "Listen with your eyes." Let us shed the limitations of self-doubt and fear and instead embrace the power of being present, engaged, and attentive. Let us look up and forward with a keen eye for the possibilities that lie ahead and a heart filled with confidence and determination to shape our own professional destinies.

Kimberly

TALENT SPOTLIGHT THEMES AND CHAPTER CROSSWALK

TALENT THEMES	THEME DESCRIPTIONS	STRONG TALENT Chapters and subthemes that may feel most intuitive, easier to implement, and more natural. Identify ways to build stronger talents by referring to these chapters and sections and note on your *Now, Near, Next Blueprint*.	SOFTER TALENT Chapters and subthemes may feel least intuitive, more difficult to implement, and less natural. Identify ways to prop up softer talents, as described in chapter four, "Architect Your Journey."
Drives and Values describe a person's motivation to develop their potential and set high expectations. This group also reflects the personal principles by which they live and work.			

Achiever	Fueled by an unstoppable drive, you spring into action and rise to meet challenges. Your accomplishments are an important source of pride, and they flow from your propensity to lead and excel, not just participate. Every challenge provides another opportunity to grow and thrive as you set new goals to push yourself.	**Chapter 4:** Architect Your Journey Authenticate Your Brand Amplify Your Aspirations **Chapter 6:** Broaden Your Perspective Stretch Your Reach Internally Widen Your View **Chapter 7:** Radiate Confidence Embolden Self-Efficacy Show Up & Speak Up **Chapter 8:** Take Risks Harness Your Fear Make Bold Moves **Chapter 9:** Bolster Resilience & Agility Celebrate Success	**Chapter 9:** Bolster Resilience & Agility Navigate Rerouting Exercise Holistic Self-Care
Purpose	Driven by deep integrity, each choice you make illuminates your dedication to principles. Rooted in trustworthiness, you move and act with conviction. Continue to lead with your sense of purpose and inspire others by consistently doing what's right and doing it exceptionally well.	**Chapter 2:** Proclaim Your Purpose Declare Core Values Develop Your Why Inspire Your Vision	**Chapter 8:** Take Risks Harness Your Fear Make Bold Moves

Work Style addresses how a person carries out their job responsibilities. Factors considered include their energy level, ability to set priorities, and capacity to plan what needs to be achieved to meet expectations.

Mastery	Every task, even the most repetitive, is executed with finesse, ensuring accurate details and nearly flawless results. Your adept command over details guarantees exceedingly low margins for error, keying into important elements others likely overlook.	**Chapter 2:** Proclaim Your Purpose Declare Core Values Develop Your Why Inspire Your Vision **Chapter 4:** Architect Your Journey Chart Your *Now, Near, Next* **Chapter 9:** Bolster Resilience & Agility Develop a Base-Camp	**Chapter 6:** Broaden Your Perspective Stretch Your Reach Internally Widen Your View **Chapter 7:** Radiate Confidence Embolden Self-Efficacy Practice Positive Self-Talk **Chapter 8:** Take Risks Harness Your Fear Make Bold Moves
Orchestrator	Flexing unparalleled efficiency and discipline, you deftly navigate complexities with ease. You possess an innate ability to transform strategy and visions into tangible milestones and ensure a path to success.	**Chapter 4:** Architect Your Journey Chart Your *Now, Near, Next* **Chapter 7:** Radiate Confidence Practice Positive Self-Talk **Chapter 9:** Bolster Resilience & Agility Develop a Base-Camp Mindset	**Chapter 9:** Bolster Resilience & Agility Navigate Rerouting

People Acumen explains how a person builds relationships with others and how others feel about their relationships with that person.

Positivity	Your optimistic attitude shines brightly in the workplace, boosting morale. By intentionally embracing positivity, you find solutions that others overlook while offsetting the drain of negativity and its effects on people's productivity and overall outlook.	**Chapter 1:** Take Charge Generate Positive Energy **Chapter 7:** Radiate Confidence Practice Positive Self-Talk **Chapter 9:** Bolster Resilience & Agility Develop a Base-Camp Mindset Navigate Rerouting Exercise Holistic Self-Care Celebrate Success	**Chapter 3:** Reveal Your Zeal Look Up, Within, and Forward!
Developer	You instinctively nurture, coach, and mentor, unlocking potential in others. Your dedication elevates performance by empowering others to flourish and grow from consistent strengths investment.	**Chapter 3:** Reveal Your Zeal Distinguish Natural Talents Alignment of Talent to Role **Chapter 5:** Recruit Supporters Appoint Your Life's BOD Engage Sponsors, Coaches, and Mentors Expand Your Network **Chapter 6:** Broaden Your Perspective Stretch Your Reach Internally Widen Your View	**Chapter 1:** Take Charge Embrace Grace Over Guilt Ask for Help

Empathetic	You thrive on the unity and fulfillment of your team, which are hallmarks of your success. Your genuine, nurturing spirit makes you an invaluable support for others.	**Chapter 3:** Reveal Your Zeal Distinguish Natural Talents Alignment of Talent to Role **Chapter 5:** Recruit Supporters Appoint Your Life's BOD Engage Sponsors, Coaches, and Mentors Expand Your Network	**Chapter 1:** Take Charge Embrace Grace Over Guilt Ask for Help **Chapter 4:** Architect Your Journey Authenticate Your Brand Amplify Your Aspirations
Personalize	You place immense value on meaningful relationships, attentively tuning into each individual's unique aspirations and values for a tailored approach.	**Chapter 3:** Reveal Your Zeal Distinguish Natural Talents Alignment of Talent to Role **Chapter 5:** Recruit Supporters Appoint Your Life's BOD Engage Sponsors, Coaches, and Mentors Expand Your Network	**Chapter 1:** Take Charge Embrace Grace Over Guilt Ask for Help **Chapter 4:** Architect Your Journey Authenticate Your Brand Amplify Your Aspirations

Influence defines how a person achieves outcomes, gets others to do something, buys into something, or works toward a common goal.

Influential	When the moment demands leadership, you confidently step up to guide the way. You make a remarkable difference by leveraging your deep conviction and shaping others' thinking as a role model.	**Chapter 1:** Take Charge Embrace Grace Over Guilt Ask for Help **Chapter 7:** Radiate Confidence Embolden Self-Efficacy Show Up & Speak Up **Chapter 8:** Take Risks Harness Your Fear Make Bold Moves	**Chapter 5:** Recruit Supporters Appoint Your Life's BOD Engage Sponsors, Coaches, and Mentors Expand Your Network **Chapter 9:** Bolster Resilience & Agility Navigate Rerouting Exercise Holistic Self-Care Celebrating Success

Thought Process describes how an individual learns through new experiences and applies the knowledge gained in different situations. This group also explains a person's talent for developing innovative ideas and problem-solving solutions.

Agility	Thriving on change, you nimbly adapt, keeping everyone aligned and on course. Your instinctive flexibility ensures projects advance seamlessly, even amidst shifts.	**Chapter 6:** Broaden Your Perspective Stretch Your Reach Internally Widen Your View **Chapter 9:** Bolster Resilience & Agility Develop a Base-Camp Mindset Navigate Rerouting Exercise Holistic Self-Care Celebrate Success	**Chapter 4:** Architect Your Journey Chart Your *Now, Near, Next*

| Strategic Impact | You astutely grasp the broader landscape, impressing and guiding others with your sharp insights. You masterfully identify overarching needs, ensuring teams and departments align for optimal outcomes. | **Chapter 2:** Proclaim Your Purpose Declare Core Values Develop Your Why Inspire Your Vision

Chapter 3: Reveal Your Zeal Distinguish Natural Talents Alignment of Talent to Role

Chapter 4: Architect Your Journey Authenticate Your Brand

Chapter 6: Broaden Your Perspective Stretch Your Reach Internally Widen Your View

Chapter 8: Take Risks Develop a Base-Camp Mindset Navigate Rerouting | **Chapter 1:** Take Charge Embrace Grace Over Guilt Ask for Help

Chapter 9: Bolster Resilience & Agility Exercise Holistic Self-Care Celebrating Success |

| Growth-Minded | You possess an insatiable thirst for knowledge, turning every interaction into a learning opportunity. Your ability to visualize and adapt allows for you to harness new insights to drive impactful outcomes. | **Chapter 3:**
Reveal Your Zeal
Look Up, Within, and Forward!
Distinguish Natural Talents
Alignment of Talent to Role

Chapter 4:
Architect Your Journey
Chart Your *Now, Near, Next*
Create a Strengths-Development Plan
Authenticate Your Brand

Chapter 6:
Broaden Your Perspective
Stretch Your Reach Internally
Widen Your View

Chapter 9:
Bolster Resilience & Agility
Develop a Base-Camp Mindset
Navigate Rerouting
Celebrating Success | **Chapter 1:**
Take Charge
Embrace Grace Over Guilt
Ask for Help |

NOTES

American Psychological Association. 2015. "Work-Life Fit Linked to Employee Engagement, Motivation, and Job Satisfaction." https://www.apa.org/news/press/releases/2015/09/work-life-fit.

Bravata, Dena M., Sharon A. Watts, Autumn L. Keefer, Divya K. Madhusudhan, Katie T. Taylor, Dani M. Clark, Ross S. Nelson, Kevin O. Cokley, and Heather K. Hagg. 2020. "Prevalence, Predictors, and Treatment of Impostor Syndrome: A Systematic Review." *Journal of General Internal Medicine* 35 (4). https://doi.org/007/s11606-019-05364-1.

Carter, Sherrie B. 2013. "Are You Overcommitted?" *Psychology Today*, November 4, 2013. https://www.psychologytoday.com/nz/blog/high-octane-women/201311/are-you-overcommitted.

Ely, Robin J. and Irene Padavic. 2020. "What's Really Holding Women Back?", *Harvard Business Review.* https://hbr.org/2020/03/whats-really-holding-women-back.

Etaugh, Claire A. 2013. "Midlife Career Transitions for Women." In *Conceptualising Women's Working Lives*, edited by Wendy Patton. Rotterdam: Sense Publishers.

Greguletz, Elena, Marjo-Riitta Diehl, and Karin Kreutzer. 2019. "Why Women Build Less Effective Networks Than Men: The Role of Structural Exclusion and Personal Hesitation." *Human Relations* 72 (7): 1234-1261. https://doi.org/10.1177/0018726718804303.

Heath, Kathryn, Jill Flynn, and Mary Davis Holt. 2014. "Women, Find Your Voice." *Harvard Business Review*. https://hbr.org/2014/06/women-find-your-voice.

Hemsley, Becky. n.d. "Breathe." *Southern Cross Review*. https://southerncrossreview.org/141/hemsley-breathe.html.

Kasser, Tim and Richard M. Ryan. 1996. "Further Examining the American Dream: Differential Correlates of Intrinsic and Extrinsic Goals." *Personality and Social Psychology Bulletin* 22 (3): 281-288. https://doi.org/10.1177/0146167296223006.

Kropp, Brian. 2021. "9 Work Trends That HR Leaders Can't Ignore in 2021." Gartner, April 26, 2021. https://www.gartner.com/smarterwithgartner/9-work-trends-that-hr-leaders-cant-ignore-in-2021.

Mayo Clinic. n.d. "Positive Thinking: Stop Negative Self-Talk to Reduce Stress." https://www.mayoclinic.org/healthy-lifestyle/stress-management/in-depth/positive-thinking/art-20043950.

Myers, Jane E., Thomas J. Sweeney, and J. Melvin Witmer. 2000. "The Wheel of Wellness Counseling for Well-Being: A Holistic Model for Treatment Planning." *Journal of Counseling & Development,* 78 (3): 251-266. https://doi.org/10.1002/j.1556-6676.2000.tb01906.x.

Narayan, Liji. 2018. "Invest in Women Employees; They Are More Loyal." HR Katha, September 18, 2018. https://www.hrkatha.com/research/invest-in-women-employees-they-are-more-loyal/.

National Institute of Mental Health. n.d. "Caring for Your Mental Health." https://www.nimh.nih.gov/health/topics/caring-for-your-mental-health.

National Sleep Foundation. n.d. "Sleep Health Topics." https://www.thensf.org/sleep-health-topics/.

Office of the U.S. Surgeon General. 2023. "Our Epidemic of Loneliness and Isolation: The U.S. Surgeon General's Advisory on the Healing Effects of Social Connection and Community." https://www.hhs.gov/sites/default/files/surgeon-general-social-connection-advisory.pdf

Player, Abigail, Georgina Randsley de Moura, Ana C. Leite, Dominic Abrams, and Fatima Tresh. 2019. "Overlooked Leadership Potential: The Preference for Leadership Potential in Job Candidates Who Are Men vs. Women." *Frontiers in Psychology* 10. https://doi.org/10.3389/fpsyg.2019.00755.

Rashmi, Kumari and Aakanksha Kataria. 2021. "Work-Life Balance: A Systematic Literature Review and Bibliometric Analysis." *International Journal of Sociology and Social Policy.* https://doi.org/10.1108/IJSSP-06-2021-0145.

Rosenberg, Joan I. 2019. *90 Seconds to a Life You Love: How to Master Your Difficult Feelings to Cultivate Lasting Confidence, Resilience, and Authenticity.* New York: Little, Brown Spark.

Sommers, M. 2022. MIT. "Women Are Less Likely Than Men to Be Promoted." https://mitsloan.mit.edu/ideas-made-to-matter/women-are-less-likely-men-to-be-promoted-heres-one-reason-why.

Torstveit, Linda, Stefan Sütterlin, and Ricardo Gregorio Lugo. 2016. "Empathy, Guilt Proneness, and Gender: Relative Contributions to Prosocial Behaviour." *Europe's Journal of Psychology* 12 (2): 187. https://doi.org/10.5964/ejop.v12i2.1097.

Turnage, Kim and Larry Sternberg. 2017. *Managing to Make a Difference: How to Engage, Retain, and Develop Talent for Maximum Performance*. Hoboken: Wiley.

U.S. Department of Labor Bureau of Labor Statistics. 2022. "Employment Characteristics of Families—2022." April 19, 2023. https://www.bls.gov/news.release/pdf/famee.pdf.

UN Women. n.d. "SDG 5: Achieve Gender Equality and Empower All Women and Girls." https://www.unwomen.org/en/node/36060.

Westervelt, Amy. 2018. *Forget "Having It All": How America Messed Up Motherhood—and How to Fix It*. New York: Seal Press.

Windley, Kris. 2019. "Don't Listen to Impostor Syndrome; You Aren't Just Anything." March 26, 2019. https://www.withakwriting.com/impostor-syndrome/.

Wu, Yvette. 2023. "Why We Need to End 'Mom Guilt' Once and for All." *Fast Company*, May 14, 2023. https://www.fastcompany.com/90895797/why-we-need-to-end-mom-guilt-once-and-for-all.

Ziegler, Sheryl G. 2020. "How to Let Go of Working-Mom Guilt." *Harvard Business Review*, September 4, 2020. https://hbr.org/2020/09/how-to-let-go-of-working-mom-guilt.

ACKNOWLEDGMENTS

To:

Our incredible families, who have supported and encouraged us throughout this journey,

The remarkable women who gave so generously of their time, talent, and wisdom in the research and development of this book,

The mentors, coaches, and sponsors that have guided, pushed, and challenged us along the way,

Our respective life's board of directors (living and passed) that have and continue to form us into the best versions of ourselves,

Our dear friends who have cheered us on and believed we could,

Kristin Olson and Heather Aimee O'Neill for their brilliant insights and edits,

Naren, Lauren, and the Amplify Publishing team for believing this was worthy work, and

My collaborator, friend, mentor, and business partner, Kimberly K. Rath, for having the passion for developing potential and enough trust in me to invest her time, talent, and treasure into bringing to life *Now, Near, Next!*

Cynthia

ABOUT THE AUTHORS

Dr. Cynthia Bentzen-Mercer, cofounder of Zeal of the Heel and founder of Bentzen Performance Partners, is a business executive, human capital strategist, author, and executive coach. Working from the time she was 14, her leadership journey began early. A working mom and breadwinner serving in predominantly male-led industries, throughout most of her 30-year career she was the youngest and only female on the executive team.

Navigating a progressive career as a chief executive in gaming, hospitality, and health-care, while raising two children and pursuing advanced degrees, Cynthia has experienced the joys and challenges of trying to "have it all." With deep appreciation for those who shined a light for her, and as a social psychologist with a passion to unleash human potential, she feels a personal responsibility to help women claim their agency and amplify their possibilities.

Kimberly Rath is a bestselling author, cofounder of Zeal of the Heel, and cofounder and cochairman of Talent Plus.® An innovator and visionary, Kimberly has been at the forefront of thinking about talent her entire career, helping others discover and develop their unique strengths. Through her leadership at Talent Plus,® she has delivered tremendous outcomes for some of the world's most well-known brands, including Estée Lauder, Ferragamo, Delta Airlines, UCLA Health, University of Kansas Health, The Ritz-Carlton, and KSL Resorts.

Kimberly is passionate about giving back, sitting on several boards, and supporting various foundations and professional organizations. Kimberly is also the *Wall Street Journal* and *USA Today* bestselling author of *Business Success Secrets*.

Step into a world of boundless possibilities with
The Zeal of the Heel

In the fast-paced world of career development, we understand
the daily challenges that organizations and associations face
when striving to empower women and help advance their
professional journeys. Work demands, caregiving roles, and
other responsibilities often leave little room to envision a more
intentional future.

We want to help women lift their gaze and see beyond the chaos
to redefine their future goals.

To book Cynthia or Kimberly for speaking engagements,
workshops, corporate consulting, or executive coaching, email
Cynthia@zealoftheheel.com.